s £6.

D1092300

MINOR PARTIES
at
BRITISH
PARLIAMENTARY
ELECTIONS
1885–1974

OTHER BOOKS IN THIS SERIES

MINOR PARTIES
at
BRITISH
PARLIAMENTARY
ELECTIONS

1885–1974

Compiled and Edited by
F.W.S. CRAIG

M

First published 1975 by
THE MACMILLAN PRESS LTD
London and Basingstoke
Associated companies in New York
Dublin Melbourne Johannesburg and Madras

SBN 333 17152 7

Typeset by
LITHOSET
Chichester

Printed in Great Britain by
THOMSON LITHO LTD
East Kilbride

CONTENTS

CONTENTS

PREFACE

During the years which I have spent compiling reference books on British elections, I have been frequently inconvenienced and frustrated by the lack of a single-volume source of background information and electoral data on the numerous small parties and organisations which have sponsored or supported parliamentary candidates since 1885. This new volume supplements the data in the *British Parliamentary Election Results* series and is an attempt to provide basic information in a compact form which should meet the needs of journalists and academics.

Coverage is confined to Great Britain (to have listed parties operating in Northern Ireland would have created the problem of including election data relating to the former Northern Ireland Parliament and Assembly as well as to the Parliament at Westminster) and 'minor party' has for the purpose of this book been defined as a party not allied or affiliated to the Conservative, Labour or Liberal parties.

In deciding what in fact constituted a 'party' as distinct from a 'one-man band' I have excluded all those 'parties' who appeared to have no organisation or membership outwith the founder and his close associates. Anyone can form a political party and in recent years there has been a proliferation of candidates standing under strange 'party' labels but this book is not concerned with the eccentric independent who decides to form a new party for election purposes.

The difficulties of obtaining *verified* information on small parties and organisations was immense. Many of them ceased activities years ago leaving only meagre records and they rarely merited coverage in the national press. In a number of instances I have been unable to confirm to my satisfaction the dates of formation or dissolution but no effort has been spared to ensure as high a standard of accuracy as has been possible with the limited and sometimes conflicting material available.

With only a few exceptions I have enjoyed the co-operation of many officials, members and former members of the organisations included in this book and I would like to express my thanks to them but at the same time emphasize that the final responsibility for each entry rested with the Editor. To those who for reasons perhaps best known to the Special Branch, either refused or were only willing to provide minimal details of their background, I can only say that I have done my best to provide an accurate entry.

As with the other books in this series, I owe a considerable debt of gratitude to my wife, Phyllis and elder daughter, Susan. Not only have they helped in the proof reading and indexing but their encouragement to complete a somewhat difficult and frustrating book was appreciated, although perhaps not always at the time.

F.W.S. CRAIG
Compiler and Editor

Parliamentary Research Services
Chichester

February 1975

INTRODUCTORY NOTES

1. Parties and organisations are listed in alphabetical order under their most recent name. The index on pages 130–32 provides references to the former names of parties.

2. The list under **Sources** is selective and includes only those books and periodicals which were considered by the Editor to be the most useful source of further reference. Periodicals which were the official or semi-official publications of the parties are indicated by an asterisk (*) preceding the title. Opening and closing dates of periodicals have been verified as far as possible from the *British Union Catalogue of Periodicals* and the catalogues of the British Library (Reference Division and Newspaper Library). Due to the fact that small parties often fail to observe the Copyright Act and do not deposit their periodicals with the Copyright libraries, the listings and dates of publication given in this book will in some cases reflect library holdings which may be incomplete.

3. Under the heading **Secessions** are listed any MPs who seceded to the party.

4. The complete parliamentary electoral activity of the party is given in chronological order under the heading **Elections**. The data is provided in six columns which contain (from left to right):
   (a) The year of the General Election (the two elections of 1910 and 1974 are distinguished by a letter code for the month) or the year and date (day/month) in the case of a by-election.

A*

(b) The constituency name in full except in the case of a county constituency where for reasons of space the county prefix has been omitted. Two and three member constituencies (except at by-elections where there was only one vacancy) are indicated by the number of seats inserted within square [2] brackets after the constituency name.

(c) The constituency reference number as used in *British Parliamentary Election Results 1885–1918; British Parliamentary Election Results 1918–1949; British Parliamentary Election Results 1950–1970; Boundaries of Parliamentary Constituencies 1885–1972.* The inclusion of this number will allow rapid reference to the full election result contained in the volumes of constituency figures which at present cover the period from 1885 to mid-1971. A further volume will probably be published in the mid-1980s taking the results through to the next major redistribution of constituency boundaries.

(d) The initials and surname of the candidate. A dagger (†) indicates a successful candidate.

(e) The number of votes polled. An asterisk (*) indicates a forfeited deposit.

(f) The number of votes polled by the candidate expressed as a percentage of the total votes cast in the constituency.

ACTION PARTY

Formed as the Union Movement by Sir Oswald Mosley in February 1948. Re-named Action Party, January 1973.

Policy   British nationalism.

Sources: Cross, Colin, *The Fascists in Britain*. 1961
                    Union, 1948—58
                    Action, 1958—64
                    National European, 1964—66
                    Action, 1966—

Elections:

1959	Kensington, North	24	Sir O.E, Mosley, Bt.	2,821*	8.1
1961 (7/11)	Manchester, Moss Side	204	W. Hesketh	1,212*	5.2
1962 (14/3)	Middlesbrough, East	209	E.J. Hamm	550*	1.8
1966	Islington, South-West	23	D.H. Harmston	816*	3.3
	Shoreditch and Finsbury	37	Sir O.E. Mosley, Bt.	1,126*	4.6
	Birmingham, Handsworth	66	E.J. Hamm	1,337*	4.1
	Manchester, Ardwick	198	F.J. Hamley	796*	2.9
1972 (7/12)	Uxbridge	446	D.H. Harmston	873*	2.5

AGRICULTURAL PARTY

Formed, as the Norfolk Farmers' Party, at a meeting of farmers addressed by Lord Beaverbrook and held at Norwich in January 1931. Re-named the Agricultural Party one week after formation.
There is no record of when the party was disbanded.

Policy:	Protection for agriculture; duties on foreign food imports; Empire free trade.
Sources:	*Daily Express*, 1931–33.

Elections:

1933 (2/2)	Fife, Eastern	592	J.L. Anderson	4,404	14.6

ALL PARTY ALLIANCE

Formed by John Creasey in 1967. In April 1973 the movement (by then known as Evolution to Democracy/All Party Alliance) merged with a body called The Organisation (formed in May 1972 and led by Colin Campion) to form the Independent Democratic Alliance (q.v.).

Policy: All party Government based on a direct proportion of the votes cast for each political party.

Sources: *Evolution to Democracy*, 1972–73
Insight, 1967–73

Elections:

1967 (9/3)	Nuneaton	507	J. Creasey	2,755*	6.4
1967 (27/4)	Brierley Hill	479	J. Creasey	1,305*	2.2
1967 (2/11)	Manchester, Gorton	203	J. Creasey	1,123*	2.7
1968 (13/6)	Oldham, West	229	J. Creasey	3,389	13.2

ANTI-PARTITION OF IRELAND LEAGUE
OF GREAT BRITAIN

Formed about 1948 as a section of the Anti-Partition of Ireland League. The League
was especially active in Glasgow, Liverpool, London and Manchester.
There is no record of when the League was disbanded.

Policy: Irish nationalism.

Sources: None traced.

Elections:

1950	Bootle	84	B. McGinnity	1,092*	2.3
	Coatbridge and Airdrie	581	T.P. O'Callaghan	1,315*	3.2
	Glasgow, Gorbals	597	W. McGuinness	1,959*	4.7
	Greenock	609	W.O. Brown[1]	718*	1.8
1951	Bootle	84	H.J. McHugh	1,340*	2.7

[1] Also advocated a policy of Scottish nationalism.

ANTI-WASTE LEAGUE

The formation of the league was announced by the *Sunday Pictorial* in January 1921. The President of the League was Viscount Rothermere and it was supported by the *Sunday Pictorial* and the *Daily Mirror*.
The League was apparently disbanded following the General Election of 1922.

Policy: To insist upon measures being taken to restore the country to solvency; urge a whole-sale reduction of expenditure; fight the battle of local rates; oppose sham Anti-Waste candidates.

Sources: *Daily Mirror*, 1921–22
Sunday Pictorial, 1921–22

Secessions: Sir T.A. Polson (Dover) who had been elected at a by-election (12/1/21) as an Independent supported by Horatio Bottomley, joined the League when it was formed. Bottomley did however continue to claim him as a member of his Independent Parliamentary Group and at the General Election of 1922 Polson ran as an Independent Conservative without the support of the League and he was defeated by an official Conservative.
Hon. E.C. Harmsworth (Isle of Thanet) who had been elected at a by-election (15/11/19) as a Conservative, joined the League when it was formed and became leader of the parliamentary group. His actions were however approved by the local Conservative Association and he remained, at least nominally, a Conservative MP and was re-elected as an official Conservative at the General Election of 1922.

Elections:

1921 (7/6)	Westminster, St. George's	59	†J.M.M. Erskine	7,244	57.5
1921 (16/6)	Hertford	356	†M.F. Sueter[1]	12,329	68.9
1921 (25/8)	Westminster, Abbey	58	R.V.K. Applin	4,970	34.9
1921 (13/9)	Lewisham, West	36	W.G. Windham	8,580	35.4

1922   At this election the League did not put forward any candidates of their own but supported the following:

Lambeth, Brixton	31	F.J. Laverack (L)	9,316	45.2
Lambeth, Kennington	32	†F.C. Harrison (C)	10,081	47.3
Lewisham, West	36	†Sir P. Dawson (C)	16,216	65.7
Paddington, South	38	E.E. Sawyer (Ind C)	4,764	32.9
Wandsworth, Putney	56	H. Higgs (L)	5,317	25.8
Westminster, St. George's	59	†J.M.M.Erskine (Ind C)	11,252	55.9
Richmond (Surrey)	212	†H.T.A.Becker (Ind C)	12,075	50.6

[1] Joint candidate of the League and Horatio Bottomley's Independent Parliamentary Group. Re-elected at the General Election of 1922 as a Conservative.

BRITISH EMPIRE PARTY

Formed by P.J. Ridout in 1951. The party appears to have been disbanded a few years later.

Policy: British nationalism.

Sources: *Bridgehead, 1951–52*

Elections:

| 1951 | Ogmore | 569 | T. David | 1,643* | 3.4 |

BRITISH MOVEMENT

Formed by Colin Jordan in May 1968. The Movement replaced the National Socialist Movement (1962–68) also formed by Jordan.

Policy: British nationalism.

Sources: *British Tidings*, 1968–

Elections:

1969 (26/6)	Birmingham, Ladywood	68	J.C.C. Jordan	282*	3.0
1970	Birmingham, Aston	62	J.C.C. Jordan	704*	2.5
1974 (F)	Wolverhampton, North-East	299	J.C.C. Jordan	711*	1.5

BRITISH NATIONAL PARTY

Formed in February 1960 as the result of the merging of the White Defence League (led by Colin Jordan) and the National Labour Party (q.v.). The party merged into the National Front (q.v.) when it was formed in March 1967.

Policy: British nationalism.

Sources: Cross, Colin, *The Fascists in Britain.* 1961
        Combat, 1960—67

Elections:

1964	Southall	263	J.E. Bean	3,410*	9.1
1966	Deptford	10	G. Rowe	1,906*	7.1
	Smethwick	262	R. Stanley	508*	1.5
	Southall	263	J.E. Bean	2,768*	7.4

BRITISH PEOPLE'S PARTY

Formed in February 1939 at a meeting in London. Viscount Tavistock (later 12th Duke of Bedford) was elected chairman and John Beckett (a former Labour MP) became Honorary Secretary. The party arose from contacts made by Viscount Lymington (later 9th Earl of Portsmouth) and John Beckett while they were publishing a monthly newspaper (owned by Viscount Lymington) called the *New Pioneer*. The party was disbanded in 1954.

Policy: When it was first formed the policy of the party was chiefly concerned with advocating social credit and pacifism. After the Second World War the party proposed a re-orientation of foreign policy, based on a recognition of national needs, as the only road to lasting peace. It also proposed a complete change in the monetary system in order to release for the country the abundance provided by scientific and mechanical progress, and the reconstruction of the agricultural life of the country with particular attention to land erosion.

Sources: *New Pioneer*, 1938–40
People's Post, 1939–54

Elections:

1939 (20/7)	Hythe	142	H. St. J.B. Philby	576*	2.6
1946 (18/3)	Combined English Universities	628	G.S. Oddie	239*	1.3

BRITISH SOCIALIST PARTY

Formed as the result of a Socialist Unity Conference held at Salford on September 30 and October 1, 1911. The initiative in forming the new party came from the Social Democratic Party which merged into the British Socialist Party along with a number of socialist societies and clubs. H.M. Hyndman and H.W. Lee who were respectively President and Secretary of the Social Democratic Party were elected to the same posts in the new party.

In January 1916 the party affiliated to the Labour Party but it merged into the Communist Party of Great Britain when it was formed in July 1920.

Policy: Revolutionary socialism.

Sources: Kendall, Walter, *The Revolutionary Movement in Britain 1900–1921.* 1969
Justice, 1911–16
The Call, 1916–20
See also the sources listed under Communist Party of Great Britain and Social Democratic Federation.

Secessions: C.J.L. Malone (Leyton, East) who had been elected as a Coalition Liberal at the General Election of 1918 joined the BSP in June 1920.

Elections:

1913 (27/6)	Leicester	128	E.R. Hartley	2,580	11.4
1913 (8/11)	Reading	163	J.G. Butler	1,063	10.4
1914 (19/2)	Tower Hamlets, Poplar	52	J.J. Jones	893	11.6

1918   At this election the BSP was affiliated to the Labour Party and of the sixteen members of the party who sought election, twelve secured the endorsement of the Labour Party (four financed by the BSP, four by local Labour parties, three by trade unions and one by the ILP) and one ran as a Co-operative Party candidate. The three BSP members who failed to secure Labour Party endorsement ran as Independent Labour or Socialist candidates. The following is a list of the sixteen BSP members:

Islington, North	26	J. Arnall[1]	4,000	19.3
Bradford, South	96	W. Hirst[2]	8,291	30.9
Edmonton	126	F.A. Broad	3,575	25.7
Great Yarmouth	130	W. McConnell	1,845	12.8
Grimsby	131	C.E. Franklin	9,015	33.7
Hastings	136	J.G. Butler	3,556	24.1
Portsmouth, Central	207	H. Hinshelwood	4,004	19.1
Salford, South	221	J. Gorman	3,807	19.0
Sheffield, Central	225	R.G. Murray[1]	643*	4.0

Sheffield, Park	229	A. Barton	3,167	20.4
Southampton [2]	232	T. Lewis	7,828	10.6
Walthamstow, West	252	V.L.T. McEntee	4,167	29.3
Glasgow, Gorbals	563	J. Maclean	7,436	34.3
Glasgow, Tradeston	573	J.D. MacDougall[1]	3,751	19.4
Greenock	574	F. Shaw	2,542*	11.2
Motherwell	603	J.T.W. Newbold	4,135	23.2

[1] Failed to obtain official Labour Party endorsement.
[2] Co-operative Party candidate.

BRITISH UNION OF FASCISTS AND
NATIONAL SOCIALISTS

Formed, as the British Union of Fascists, by Sir Oswald Mosley, in October 1932. Re-named British Union of Fascists and National Socialists in the summer of 1936. In May 1940, Mosley and other leading members of the movement were detained under the Emergency Powers Defence Regulations and in July the Regulations were again used to suspend the activities of the British Union and ban its publications for the period of the war.

Policy: Fascism and national socialism.

Sources: Cross, Colin, *The Fascists in Britain.* 1961
                  Benewick, Robert, *The Fascist Movement in Britain.* 1972
                  Action, 1936—40.
                  Blackshirt, 1933—39
                  British Union Quarterly, 1937—40
                  Fascist Quarterly, 1935—36
                  Fascist Week, 1933—34

Elections:

1940 (22/2)	West Ham, Silvertown	259	T.P. Moran	151*	1.0
1940 (13/3)	Leeds, North-East	154	S. Allen	722*	2.9
1940 (22/5)	Middleton and Prestwich	384	F. Haslam	418*	1.3

CAMPAIGN FOR SOCIAL DEMOCRACY

Formed by Dick Taverne (Democratic Labour MP for Lincoln) in September 1973.

Policy: To build a radical non-doctrinaire social democratic movement which would include the moderate members of the Labour Party.

Sources: Taverne, Dick, *The Future of the Left: Lincoln and After.* 1974
The Times, 1973–74

Elections:

1974 (F)	Haringey, Tottenham	42	J. Martin	763*	2.4
	Bristol, South-East	135	J.H. Robertson	668*	1.2
	Keighley	183	J. Binns	348*	0.8
	Lincoln	197	†D. Taverne[1]	14,780	35.6
	Penistone	511	M. Eaden	867*	1.6
1974 (O)	Lincoln	197	D. Taverne[1]	13,714	34.6

[1] Although Taverne was the founder of the Campaign for Social Democracy, his candidature was on each occasion sponsored by the Lincoln Democratic Labour Association who were not formally linked to the CSD although they supported the latters' principals and aims.

COMMON WEALTH

Formed at a conference in London in July 1942 when the Forward March movement (led by Sir Richard Acland, Liberal MP for Barnstaple) and the 1941 Committee (led by J.B. Priestley) merged to form a new political organisation. In September 1945 Sir Richard Acland resigned from the movement and shortly afterwards it ceased most of its activities, continuing only as a discussion group. There are probably still some local groups in existence.

Policy: Socialism founded on Christian morality.

Sources: Acland, Sir Richard, *The Forward March.* 1941
Acland, Sir Richard, *What it will be Like in the New Britain.* 1942
Acland, Sir Richard, *How it Can be Done.* 1943
Calder, A.L.R., *The Common Wealth Party, 1942–45.* D. Phil. Thesis, University of Sussex, Brighton. 1968
Wintringham, Tom, *The People's War.* 1942
Common Wealth Information Bulletin, 1943–46
Common Wealth Review, 1944–49
CW News-Letter, 1950–54

Secessions: Sir Richard Acland (Barnstaple) who had been elected as a Liberal at the General Election of 1935, was a co-founder of Common Wealth and resigned from the Liberal Party in September 1942.

Elections:

Date	Constituency		Candidate	Votes	%
1943 (10/2)	Ashford	363	Mrs. C.E. Williamson	4,192	30.3
1943 (11/12)	Midlothian and Peeblesshire, Northern	607	T.H. Wintringham	10,751	48.1
1943 (16/2)	Portsmouth, North	208	T. Sargant	4,545	40.3
1943 (23/2)	Watford	359	A.R. Blackburn	11,838	46.1
1943 (7/4)	Eddisbury	287	†J.E. Loverseed[1]	8,023	43.7
1943 (20/4)	Daventry	419	D.G. Webb	6,591	33.4
1943 (1/6)	The Hartlepools	135	Miss E.F. Burton	3,634	17.4
1943 (8/6)	Newark	429	E.W. Moeran	3,189	13.9
1943 (9/6)	Birmingham, Aston	74	G. Hall	1,886	21.6
1944 (7/1)	Skipton	509	†H.M. Lawson	12,222	44.9
1944 (8/7)	Manchester, Rusholme	184	H. Blomerley	6,670	42.1
1945 (26/4)	Chelmsford	332	†E.R. Millington	24,548	57.5
1945	Chelsea	11	Dr. Dorothy A Sharpe	984*	5.2
	Wandsworth, Putney	56	Sir R.T.D. Acland, Bt.	2,686*	8.0
	Westminster, St. George's	59	W.B.D. Brown	5,314	27.3
	Harrow, West	134	H.M. Lawson	2,462*	4.3
	Newcastle upon Tyne, North	194	H.A.C. Ridsdale	904*	2.6

Plymouth, Drake	205	E.J. Trout	1,681*	5.7
Richmond (Surrey)	212	D.G.H. Frank	753*	1.7
Sheffield, Ecclesall	226	S. Checkland	12,045	35.9
Wimbledon	265	K.E. Horne	2,472*	3.6
Newbury	276	G.B. Suggett	424*	0.9
Knutsford	288	F.W. Young	628*	1.1
Chelmsford	332	†E.R. Millington[2]	27,309	46.7
Aldershot	346	T.H. Wintringham	14,435	42.6
Petersfield	350	T. Sargant	6,600	18.5
Canterbury	364	Mrs. C.E. Williamson	1,017*	2.6
Fylde	379	K.E. Heath	1,784*	2.9
Bury St. Edmunds	453	E.C.G. England	750*	2.4
Sutton Coldfield	474	Mrs. J. Purser	2,043*	4.2
Evesham	484	D.L. Donnelly	7,727	23.1
Richmond (Yorks)	491	R.N. Chesterton	813*	2.3
Thirsk and Malton	493	E.W. Moeran	13,572	39.9
Glasgow, Pollok	569	W.J. Voisey-Youldon	932*	2.9
Midlothian and Peeblesshire, Northern	607	Mrs. K. Wintringham	3,299*	6.4

[1] Resigned from Common Wealth in November 1944 and joined the Labour Party, May 1945. Defeated at the General Election of 1945.

[2] Resigned from Common Wealth and joined the Labour Party, April 1946. Defeated at the General Election of 1950.

COMMONWEALTH LAND PARTY

Formed, as the Commonwealth League, in January 1919 by J.W.G. Peace. Re-named the Commonwealth Land Party in September 1923. After Peace's death in April 1947, the party was re-named the Common Land Party. There is no record of the party being active after 1950 and it is likely that it has been disbanded.

Policy: The restoration of the land to the people.

Sources: *Commonweal,* 1919–34, 1939–41, 1948–50

Elections:

1931	Stoke-on-Trent, Burslem	238	A. Rowland-Entwistle	401*	1.1
	Stoke-on-Trent, Hanley	239	J.W.G. Peace	946*	2.7

COMMUNIST PARTY OF ENGLAND (MARXIST-LENINIST)

Formed in March 1972. The party had its origins in an organisation called the English Internationalists which was formed in August 1967 by Hardial Bains who had founded the first branch of the "Internationalists" in March 1963 at the University of British Columbia, Vancouver, Canada.

Policy: Communism (Maoist).

Sources: *Communist England,* 1973–
             Workers' Weekly, 1971–72
             Workers' Daily, 1972–

Elections:

1973 (27/6)	Manchester, Exchange	202	Miss R. Pushkin	109*	1.1
1973 (8/11)	Hove	159	Mrs. C. Reakes	128*	0.3
1974 (F)	Lambeth, Central	62	E.D. Brome	107*	0.4
	Wandsworth, Battersea, North	89	Mrs. C. Reakes	208*	0.7
	Birmingham, Handsworth	107	Miss S. Thompson	334*	1.0
	Brighton, Kemptown	130	J.C. Buckle	170*	0.3
	Manchester, Moss Side	212	Miss R. Pushkin	206*	0.6
	Portsmouth, South	241	A.D. Rifkin	394*	0.7
1974 (O)	Lambeth, Central	62	P.J. Bratton	88*	0.3
	Wandsworth, Battersea, North	89	Mrs. C. Reakes	102*	0.4
	Birmingham, Handsworth	107	J.L. Hutchinson	103*	0.3
	Brighton, Kemptown	130	J.C. Buckle	125*	0.3
	Bristol, South-East	135	P. Rowe	79*	0.1
	Leicester, South	194	G.H. Rousseau	136*	0.3
	Portsmouth, South	241	A.D. Rifkin	612*	1.2
	Cardiff, South-East	520	B.C.D. Harris	75*	0.2

COMMUNIST PARTY OF GREAT BRITAIN

Formed at a Unity Convention held in London on July 31 and August 1, 1920. The convention was attended by about 160 delegates of whom 96 represented branches of the British Socialist Party which had previously agreed to merge into the new party. The party affiliated to the Third (Communist) International.

Policy:	Communism.

Sources: Bell, Tom, *The Communist Party: A Short History.* 1937
Klugmann, James, *History of the Communist Party of Great Britain.*
  Volume One: Formation and Early Years, 1919–1924. 1968
Klugmann, James, *History of the Communist Party of Great Britain.*
  Volume Two: The General Strike, 1925–1927. 1969
Macfarlane, L.J., *The British Communist Party: Its Origins and Development until 1929.* 1966
Pearce, Brian, *Early History of the Communist Party of Great Britain.* 1966
Pelling, Henry, *The British Communist Party: A Historical Profile.* 1958
*Communist, 1920–23 and 1927–28
*Communist Review, 1921–27 and 1929–35
*Daily Worker, 1930–66
*Morning Star, 1966–
*Workers' Weekly, 1923–27

Secessions: C.J.L. Malone (Leyton, East) who had been elected as a Coalition Liberal at the General Election of 1918 joined the British Socialist Party in 1920 and then the Communist Party when it was formed. He did not seek re-election at the General Election of 1922 and subsequently joined the Labour Party.

Elections:

1922 (24/8)	Caerphilly	534	R. Stewart	2,592*	10.3
1922[1]	Bethnal Green, North-East	5	W. Windsor	5,659	35.3
	Bethnal Green, South-West	6	J.J. Vaughan	4,034	31.9
	Dundee [2]	552	W. Gallacher	5,906*	5.0
	Greenock	574	A. Geddes	9,776	34.1
	Motherwell	603	†J.T.W. Newbold	8,262	33.3
1923[1]	Dundee [2]	552	W. Gallacher	10,380	10.1
	Glasgow, Kelvingrove	566	A. Ferguson	10,021	39.0
	Greenock	574	A. Geddes	10,335	38.7
	Motherwell	603	J.T.W. Newbold	8,712	37.4
1924	Battersea, North	1	†S. Saklatvala	15,096	50.9
	Bethnal Green, South-West	6	J.J. Vaughan	6,024	40.9
	Wandsworth, Streatham	57	A.M. Wall	3,204	13.8
	Birmingham, West	84	Dr. R. Dunstan	7,158	32.6

	Manchester, Rusholme	184	W. Paul	5,328	20.2
	Nottingham, East	199	T. Mann	2,606*	10.8
	Dundee [2]	552	R. Stewart	8,340	6.7
	Greenock	574	A. Geddes	7,590	29.0
1928 (16/8)	Aberdeen, North	548	A. Ferguson	2,618	12.9
1929	Battersea, North	1	S. Saklatvala	6,554	18.6
	Bethnal Green, South-West	6	Dr. R. Dunstan	1,368*	7.7
	Hackney, South	20	J.T. Murphy	331*	1.1
	Stepney, Limehouse	49	W.T.L. Tapsell	245*	1.0
	Manchester, Platting	183	J.J. Vaughan	401*	1.0
	Sheffield, Attercliffe	223	G.H. Fletcher	1,731*	5.5
	Tottenham, South	244	H.T.W. Sara	490*	1.6
	Wallsend	249	W. Hannington	744*	1.8
	Wigan	262	F. Bright	1,307*	2.8
	Seaham	329	H. Pollitt	1,431*	2.9
	Mansfield	428	Miss R. Smith	533*	1.1
	Spen Valley	511	S. Usmani	242*	0.6
	Rhondda, East	520	A.L. Horner	5,789	15.2
	Caerphilly	534	J.R. Wilson	829*	2.3
	Ogmore	538	J.R. Campbell	1,525*	3.8
	Aberdeen, North	548	A. Ferguson	1,686*	5.8
	Dundee [2]	552	R. Stewart	6,160*	3.6
	Dunfermline Burghs	553	J.V. Leckie	1,712*	6.5
	Glasgow, St. Rollox	570	G.W. Middleton	613*	1.9
	Greenock	574	A. Geddes	7,005	20.4
	Fife, Western	593	W. Gallacher	6,040	20.5
	Bothwell	599	Mrs. H. Crawfurd	1,677*	5.5
	Hamilton	601	F. Moore	395*	1.6
	Motherwell	603	Mrs. I. Brown	984*	3.4
	Rutherglen	605	A.B. Moffat	842*	2.5
1929 (1/8)	Leeds, South-East	156	W.T.E. Brain	512*	4.2
1929 (27/11)	Kilmarnock	585	Mrs. I. Brown	1,448*	4.4
1930 (6/2)	Sheffield, Brightside	224	J.T. Murphy	1,084*	4.4
1930 (26/6)	Glasgow, Shettleston	571	S. Saklatvala	1,459*	5.8
1930 (6/11)	Shipley	508	W. Gallacher	701*	1.7
1930 (3/12)	Stepney, Whitechapel and St. George's	51	H. Pollitt	2,106*	9.6
1931 (19/5)	Ogmore	538	J.R. Campbell	5,219	21.2
1931	Battersea, North	1	S. Saklatvala	3,021*	9.0
	Bermondsey, West	4	W. Hannington	873*	4.2
	Bethnal Green, South-West	6	J.J. Vaughan	2,970	17.4

Communist Party of Great Britain

1931	Greenwich	17	Mrs. K.S. Duncan	2,024*	4.5
(cont.)	Hammersmith, North	21	E.F. Bramley	697*	2.2
	St. Pancras, North	42	W.G. Shepherd	456*	1.3
	St. Pancras, South-East	43	S. Usmani	332*	1.2
	Stepney, Whitechapel and				
	St. George's	51	H. Pollitt	2,658*	11.2
	Birmingham, Duddeston	76	B. Moore	327*	1.2
	Burnley	104	J. Rushton	512*	0.8
	Liverpool, Scotland	171	L.J. McGree	1,544*	5.6
	Manchester, Gorton	180	C. Flanagan	1,000*	2.6
	Sheffield, Attercliffe	223	G.H. Fletcher	2,790*	8.5
	Sheffield, Brightside	224	J.T. Murphy	1,571*	4.1
	Seaham	329	G. Lumley	677*	1.3
	Rhondda, East	520	A.L. Horner	10,359	31.9
	Rhondda, West	521	J.L. Davies	4,296	15.7
	Ogmore	538	J.R. Campbell	3,099*	8.2
	Aberdeen, North	548	Mrs. H. Crawfurd	3,980*	11.2
	Dundee [2]	552	R. Stewart	10,264*	5.8
	Edinburgh, Central	554	F. Douglas	1,319*	4.5
	Glasgow, Gorbals	563	H. McShane	2,626*	7.9
	Glasgow, Springburn	572	A. Haimes	1,997*	5.8
	Greenock	574	A. Ferguson	6,440	18.2
	Fife, Western	593	W. Gallacher	6,829	22.1
	Bothwell	599	B. McCourt	2,163*	6.5
1932 (17/3)	Dunbartonshire	591	H. McIntyre	2,870*	7.5
1933 (28/3)	Rhondda, East	520	A.L. Horner	11,228	33.8
1933 (1/9)	Clay Cross	304	H. Pollitt	3,434*	10.8
1933 (7/11)	Skipton	509	J. Rushton	704*	1.7
1934 (24/4)	Hammersmith, North	21	E.F. Bramley	614*	2.4
1934 (5/6)	Merthyr Tydfil, Merthyr	518	W. Hannington	3,409*	9.5
1935	Rhondda, East	520	H. Pollitt	13,655	38.2
	Fife, Western	593	†W. Gallacher	13,462	37.4
1939 (8/12)	Stretford	389	E.A. Gower	1,519*	5.2
1940 (22/2)	West Ham, Silvertown	259	H. Pollitt	966*	6.2
1940 (12/6)	Poplar, Bow and Bromley	39	Mrs. I. Brown	506*	4.2
1941 (27/2)	Dunbartonshire	591	M. MacEwen	3,862	15.0
1945	Hackney, South	20	W. Rust	4,891	24.2
	Stepney, Mile End	50	†P. Piratin	5,075	47.6
	Westminster, Abbey	58	G. Carritt	2,964	17.6
	Birmingham, Handsworth	79	Mrs. J. Eden	1,390*	3.4
	Birmingham, Sparkbrook	83	R.P. Dutt	1,853*	7.6
	Coventry, East	110	W. Alexander	3,986*	7.0

	Harrow, East	133	Miss G.M. Driver	3,493*	5.9
	Hornsey	140	G.J. Jones	10,058	21.5
	Preston [2]	210	P.J. Devine	5,168*	3.8
	Rossendale	217	W. Whittaker	1,663*	4.6
	Sheffield, Brightside	224	H. Hill	4,115	13.0
	Sheffield, Hallam	227	G.H. Cree	2,253*	6.7
	Sunderland [2]	241	T.A. Richardson	4,501*	3.3
	Abingdon	275	J.C.D. Dunman	1,668*	4.4
	Sevenoaks	373	K.F. Thompson	676*	1.6
	Rhondda, East	520	H. Pollitt	15,761	45.5
	Glasgow, Central	562	R.H. Cooney	2,709	12.7
	Glasgow, Shettleston	571	P. Kerrigan	4,122*	12.3
	Greenock	574	J.R. Campbell	5,900	17.2
	Kirkcaldy Burghs	575	J. McArthur	2,898*	8.5
	Fife, Western	593	†W. Gallacher	17,636	42.1
1948 (4/3)	Wigan	262	T. Rowlandson	1,647*	3.4
1948 (30/9)	Glasgow, Gorbals	563	P. Kerrigan	4,233	16.9
1949 (10/3)	St. Pancras, North	42	J. Mahon	854*	3.0
1950	Battersea, North	2	J. Mahon	655*	1.8
	Bethnal Green	5	J.J. Mildwater	610*	1.9
	Camberwell, Peckham	7	T.R. Gibson	886*	1.8
	Cities of London and Westminster	9	G. Carritt	888*	1.7
	Deptford	10	L.F. Stannard	562*	1.3
	Fulham, East	12	R.E. Elsmere	399*	1.1
	Hackney, South	16	J.R. Betteridge	2,199*	3.7
	Hampstead	19	W.R.T. Gore	1,603*	2.8
	Islington, South-West	23	A. Bender	834*	1.8
	Kensington, North	24	J.L.R. Eyre	551*	1.3
	Lambeth, Vauxhall	28	Miss M.C. Heinemann	508*	1.3
	Lewisham, South	30	J.W. Jones	635*	1.3
	Paddington, North	32	D. Cohen	417*	1.2
	Poplar	34	H. Watson	540*	1.4
	St. Pancras, North	36	T. Ahern	967*	1.8
	Southwark	38	S.P. Bent	668*	1.3
	Stepney	39	P. Piratin	5,991	12.5
	Wandsworth, Clapham	42	Mrs. G. Draper	619*	1.3
	Woolwich, East	45	R.P. Dutt	601*	1.4
	Acton	48	A.F. Papworth	663*	1.5
	Ashton-under-Lyne	50	H.H.H. Blackwell	459*	1.1
	Bexley	58	C.C. Job	481*	0.9
	Birkenhead	60	S. Coulthard	971*	1.8

22

Communist Party of Great Britain

1950					
(cont.)	Birmingham, Northfield	69	R.A. Etheridge	479*	0.9
	Birmingham, Sparkbrook	73	J.W. Crump	355*	0.9
	Birmingham, Yardley	75	J. Falconer	347*	0.8
	Bradford, East	88	H.G. Green	543*	1.2
	Brentford and Chiswick	92	J.H. Parker	401*	1.0
	Bristol, South-East	100	J.F. Webb	524*	1.1
	Burnley	103	W. Whittaker	526*	1.0
	Chesterfield	108	B. Barker	554*	1.0
	Coventry, East	109	W. Alexander	487*	0.9
	Croydon, West	118	R. Jarvie	336*	0.7
	Dagenham	119	G.T. Bridges	883*	1.5
	East Ham, South	131	E.C.W. Thomas	401*	1.1
	Eton and Slough	137	P.L.N. Smith	614*	1.5
	Harrow, East	149	W.O. Seaman	633*	1.2
	Hayes and Harlington	153	F.T. Foster	573*	1.5
	Hendon, North	154	Mrs. M.E. Pollitt	918*	2.0
	Hornsey	158	G.J. Jones	1,191*	1.9
	Ilford, South	163	D. Kelly	913*	1.6
	Leeds, North-East	176	B. Ramelson	612*	1.5
	Leicester, North-East	181	F.C. Westacott	327*	0.7
	Liverpool, Scotland	192	J. Coward	615*	1.4
	Manchester, Blackley	199	B. Ainley	562*	1.1
	Manchester, Gorton	203	S. Abbott	873*	1.7
	Manchester, Wythenshawe	207	Miss F. Dean	588*	1.3
	Middlesbrough, East	209	Dr. N. Levy	367*	0.8
	Newcastle upon Tyne, West	217	R. McNair	492*	0.9
	Nottingham, North-West	224	A. West	719*	1.5
	Oldham, West	229	W. Maudsley	438*	0.9
	Oxford	230	E. Keeling	494*	0.8
	Portsmouth, West	237	G.H. Swanton	257*	0.5
	Preston, North	238	P.J. Devine	366*	0.8
	Sheffield, Brightside	256	H. Hill	1,081*	2.3
	Sheffield, Hillsborough	259	M. Bennett	759*	1.5
	Sheffield, Park	261	A. Fullard	909*	2.0
	Southall	263	J.A. Purton	839*	1.7
	South Shields	270	F.O. Smith	415*	0.7
	Swindon	283	I. Gradwell	295*	0.7
	Tottenham	285	G.R. Cross	802*	1.5
	Warrington	297	J.J. Grady	496*	1.1
	Wembley, South	301	N.W.H. Gill	430*	1.0
	West Ham, South	304	W.J.F. Norris	730*	1.6
	Wigan	305	T. Rowlandson	1,243*	2.4

	Willesden, West	307	D.A. Michaelson	938*	1.7
	Woodford	311	W.G.P. Brooks	827*	1.3
	Bedford	316	Mrs. E.L. Matthews	207*	0.4
	Abingdon	319	J.C.D. Dunman	396*	0.9
	Wycombe	326	Mrs. E.R. Leigh	199*	0.4
	Stalybridge and Hyde	336	D.P. Herrick	389*	0.8
	Totnes	358	E.P. Tapscott	423*	0.8
	Cirencester and Tewkesbury	382	Hon. W. Philipps	423*	0.9
	Dover	409	R.T. Morrison	474*	0.9
	Huyton	423	L.J. McGree	387*	0.9
	Kettering	453	L.P. O'Connor	368*	0.6
	Mansfield	464	W.L. Ellis	482*	0.9
	Eye	486	Mrs. D.P. Chadwick	271*	0.6
	Don Valley	532	S. Taylor	1,007*	1.9
	Shipley	540	L.T. Robb	273*	0.7
	Aberdare	543	Dr. A.T.M. Wilson	1,382*	3.1
	Rhondda, East	549	H. Pollitt	4,463	12.7
	Neath	568	A.C. Thomas	1,584*	3.5
	Ogmore	569	Miss M. Llewellyn	1,619*	3.4
	Aberdeen, North	579	R.H. Cooney	1,391*	2.7
	Dundee, East	582	D.P. Bowman	1,093*	2.2
	Edinburgh, Central	585	D.F. Renton	646*	1.9
	Glasgow, Bridgeton	592	D. Kelly	858*	2.5
	Glasgow, Gorbals	597	P. Kerrigan	2,435*	5.9
	Glasgow, Govan	598	W. Lauchlan	1,547*	3.7
	Glasgow, Scotstoun	604	R. McIlhone	1,088*	2.6
	Glasgow, Shettleston	605	M. MacEwen	1,678*	4.1
	Glasgow, Springburn	606	R.F. Horne	1,764*	4.1
	Greenock	609	J.R. Campbell	1,228*	3.0
	Stirling and Falkirk Burghs	612	G. McAlister	801*	1.8
	Kilmarnock	621	Mrs. I. Brown	860*	2.2
	Dunbartonshire, West	628	F. Hart	1,198*	2.9
	Fife, West	630	W. Gallacher	9,301	21.6
	Motherwell	638	R.B. Henderson	1,007*	2.4
	West Lothian	653	J. Borrowman	664*	1.5
1950 (5/4)	Sheffield, Neepsend	260	E.L. Moore	729*	2.3
1951	Hackney, South	16	J.R. Betteridge	1,744*	3.0
	Lewisham, South	30	J. Mahon	578*	1.2
	Stepney	39	E.F. Bramley	3,436*	7.3
	Sheffield, Brightside	256	H. Hill	1,116*	2.5
	Woodford	311	J.R. Campbell	871*	1.3
	Rhondda, East	549	I. Cox	2,948*	8.6

Communist Party of Great Britain

1951	Dundee, West	583	D.P. Bowman	1,508*	2.7
(cont.)	Glasgow, Gorbals	597	P. Kerrigan	2,553*	6.2
	Dunbartonshire, East	627	A.E. Henderson	2,158*	4.1
	Fife, West	630	W. Lauchlan	4,728*	10.5
1954 (14/4)	Motherwell	638	J. Gollan	1,457*	4.3
1955	Hackney, Central	15	J.R. Betteridge	1,530*	3.5
	St. Pancras, North	36	J. Nicolson	1,303*	3.0
	Southwark	38	S.P. Bent	959*	2.4
	Stepney	39	S. Kaye	2,888*	7.6
	Stoke Newington and Hackney North	40	A. Morris	1,525*	3.4
	Birmingham, Perry Barr	70	H. Pearce	928*	2.5
	Hayes and Harlington	153	F.T. Foster	886*	2.6
	Hornsey	158	G.J. Jones	1,442*	2.6
	Nottingham, North	223	J.H. Peck	916*	1.9
	Sheffield, Brightside	256	H. Hill	1,461*	3.5
	Wigan	305	T. Rowlandson	1,567*	3.4
	Rhondda, East	549	Mrs. A. Powell	4,544	15.1
	Dundee, West	583	D.P. Bowman	1,335*	2.6
	Glasgow, Gorbals	597	P. Kerrigan	2,491*	6.8
	Glasgow, Springburn	606	F. Hart	1,532*	5.5
	Dunbartonshire, East	627	A.E. Henderson	2,448*	4.9
	Fife, West	630	W. Lauchlan	5,389	12.6
1958 (12/6)	Wigan	305	M. Weaver	972*	2.5
1959	St. Pancras, North	36	J. Nicolson	1,230*	3.0
	Southwark	38	S.P. Bent	1,395*	3.6
	Stepney	39	S. Kaye	2,548*	6.7
	Birmingham, Perry Barr	70	H. Pearce	424*	1.1
	Hayes and Harlington	153	F.T. Foster	527*	1.4
	Hornsey	158	G.J. Jones	1,107*	2.0
	Nottingham, North	223	J.H. Peck	1,331*	2.0
	Sheffield, Brightside	256	H. Hill	1,373*	3.3
	Wigan	305	M. Weaver	945*	2.0
	Willesden, West	307	L.G. Burt	1,324*	2.9
	Rhondda, East	549	Mrs. A. Powell	4,580	14.5
	Neath	568	J.J. David	1,962*	4.6
	Dundee, West	583	D.P. Bowman	1,086*	2.1
	Glasgow, Gorbals	597	P. Kerrigan	1,932*	5.9
	Glasgow, Govan	598	G. McLennan	1,869*	4.9
	Glasgow, Springburn	606	F. Hart	1,235*	4.5
	Dunbartonshire, East	627	A.E. Henderson	2,200*	4.0
	Fife, West	630	W. Lauchlan	3,828*	8.4

1962 (14/6)	West Lothian	653	G. McLennan	1,511*	3.6
1963 (28/3)	Swansea, East	551	H. Pearce	773*	2.5
1963 (20/6)	Leeds, South	178	B. Ramelson	670*	2.2
1963 (7/11)	Luton	197	Dr. A.P.J. Chater	490*	1.1
1963 (21/11)	Dundee, West	583	D.P. Bowman	1,170*	2.6
1963 (5/12)	Manchester, Openshaw	205	E. Marsden	1,185*	4.9
1964	Battersea, North	2	Mrs. G.M. Easton	471*	2.0
	Islington, South-West	23	J.F. Moss	1,377*	5.1
	St. Pancras, North	36	J. Nicolson	1,140*	3.4
	Southwark	38	S.P. Bent	1,599*	4.9
	Stepney	39	S. Kaye	2,454*	7.9
	Birmingham, Small Heath	72	G. Jelf	926*	3.3
	Coventry, East	109	H. Bourne	1,138*	1.9
	Dagenham	119	K. Halpin	1,070*	2.1
	Hayes and Harlington	153	F. Stanley	873*	2.6
	Hornsey	158	M. Morris	1,258*	2.6
	Leeds, South	178	B. Ramelson	928*	2.6
	Liverpool, Scotland	192	T.E. Cassin	725*	2.8
	Luton	197	Dr. A.P.J. Chater	567*	1.2
	Manchester, Openshaw	205	E. Marsden	1,947*	5.1
	Mitcham	211	S.E. French	657*	1.2
	Newcastle upon Tyne, Central	214	T.G. Welch	532*	1.8
	Nottingham, North	223	J.H. Peck	1,579*	3.1
	Sheffield, Brightside	256	H. Hill	1,356*	3.5
	Swindon	283	I. Gradwell	944*	2.1
	Wigan	305	M. Weaver	988*	2.4
	Willesden, West	307	L.G. Burt	1,130*	3.0
	Goole	533	W. Carr	1,165*	2.8
	Rhondda, East	549	Mrs. A. Powell	3,385*	11.8
	Llanelli	559	R.E. Hitchon	1,061*	2.1
	Aberavon	564	Dr. J.T. Hart	1,260*	2.7
	Neath	568	J.J. David	2,342*	5.8
	Pontypool	576	W.E. Jones	1,329*	3.6
	Dundee, West	583	D.P. Bowman	1,228*	2.4
	Glasgow, Gorbals	597	Mrs. M.A. Hunter	1,339*	5.6
	Glasgow, Govan	598	G. McLennan	1,378*	4.4
	Glasgow, Springburn	606	N. McLellan	950*	3.7
	Dunbartonshire, East	627	J. Reid	1,771*	3.0
	Fife, West	630	W. Lauchlan	3,273*	7.4
	Motherwell	638	J.W. Sneddon	1,565*	3.9
	Kinross and West Perthshire	645	C.M. Grieve	127*	0.5
	West Lothian	653	Mrs. I. Swan	610*	1.2

Communist Party of Great Britain

1966					
Battersea, North	2	Mrs. G.M. Easton	650*	3.0
Fulham	11	P.T. Robson	256*	0.7
Islington, South-West	23	J.F. Moss	756*	3.0
St. Pancras, North	36	J. Nicolson	1,253*	3.8
Southwark	38	S.P. Bent	1,404*	4.7
Stepney	39	S. Kaye	2,209*	7.3
Stoke Newington and Hackney North	40	M. Goldman	1,491*	4.1
Birkenhead	60	A.B. Williams	604*	1.5
Birmingham, Northfield	69	D.W. Robinson	1,029*	1.6
Birmingham, Small Heath	72	G. Jelf	477*	1.8
Birmingham, Stechford	74	W.A.J. Dunn	998*	2.6
Bristol, North-West	98	B. Underwood	595*	1.2
Coventry, East	109	H. Bourne	1,368*	2.3
Dagenham	119	G.C. Wake	1,373*	2.9
Eccles	132	M.R. Bennett	1,239*	2.9
Erith and Crayford	136	L.H. Smith	556*	1.3
Hayes and Harlington	153	F. Stanley	698*	2.1
Hornsey	158	M. Morris	1,184*	2.5
Leeds, South	178	B. Ramelson	714*	2.1
Liverpool, Scotland	192	T.E. Cassin	779*	3.9
Luton	197	Dr. A.P.J. Chater	586*	1.2
Manchester, Openshaw	205	E. Marsden	1,479*	4.3
Mitcham	211	S.E. French	580*	1.1
Newcastle upon Tyne, Central	214	T.G. Welch	404*	1.6
Nottingham, North	223	J.H. Peck	1,070*	2.1
Sheffield, Brightside	256	H. Hill	989*	2.8
Sheffield, Park	261	C. Morton	1,002*	3.3
Stockton-on-Tees	273	E. Jones	710*	1.8
Stoke-on-Trent, South	276	S.J. Lomas	2,262*	5.1
Swindon	283	I. Gradwell	838*	2.0
Wigan	305	M. Weaver	858*	2.2
Willesden, West	307	L.G. Burt	1,140*	3.1
Mansfield	464	F.C. Westacott	590*	1.3
Goole	533	W. Carr	952*	2.3
Aberdare	543	Dr. A.T.M. Wilson	2,305*	6.4
Rhondda, East	549	Mrs. A. Powell	2,349*	8.4
Rhondda, West	550	A. True	1,853*	7.4
Swansea, East	551	W.R. Jones	902*	2.2
Llanelli	559	R.E. Hitchon	1,211*	2.6
Aberavon	564	Dr. J.T. Hart	1,620*	3.6

	Neath	568	J.J. David	1,632*	4.2
	Pontypool	576	W.E. Jones	897*	2.5
	Aberdeen, North	579	Mrs. M. Rose	719*	1.7
	Dundee, West	583	D.P. Bowman	1,217*	2.4
	Edinburgh, Leith	587	Miss H.M. Arundel	279*	1.0
	Glasgow, Gorbals	597	Mrs. M.A. Hunter	819*	4.1
	Glasgow, Govan	598	G. McLennan	1,103*	4.0
	Glasgow, Provan	603	J. Jackson	988*	2.3
	Glasgow, Scotstoun	604	H.D. Boyd	2,395*	5.4
	Glasgow, Springburn	606	N. McLellan	867*	3.7
	Greenock	609	W. Dunn	702*	2.1
	Stirling and Falkirk Burghs	612	P.J. McIntosh	767*	1.7
	Dunbartonshire, East	627	J. Reid	1,548*	2.4
	Fife, West	630	A.D. MacMillan	1,542*	3.6
	Bothwell	635	T. Woods	1,209*	2.7
	Motherwell	638	J.W. Sneddon	1,508*	4.0
	West Lothian	653	Mrs. I. Swan	567*	1.1
1967 (9/3)	Rhondda, West	550	A. True	1,723*	6.8
1967 (9/3)	Glasgow, Pollok	602	A.C. Murray	694*	1.8
1967 (2/11)	Manchester, Gorton	203	V.T. Eddisford	437*	1.0
1968 (13/6)	Sheffield, Brightside	256	R.R. Wilkinson	1,069*	4.2
1969 (30/10)	Swindon	283	Miss J. Gradwell	518*	1.3
1969 (30/10)	Glasgow, Gorbals	597	J.R. Kay	361*	2.5
1970	Battersea, North	2	D.J. Welsh	179*	1.0
	Islington, South-West	23	Mrs. M. Betteridge	509*	2.4
	St. Pancras, North	36	G. McLennan	670*	2.4
	Southwark	38	E. Hume	1,128*	4.5
	Stepney	39	S. Kaye	1,468*	5.8
	Stoke Newington and Hackney North	40	M. Goldman	793*	2.4
	Acton	48	M.W. Costin	258*	0.9
	Birkenhead	60	A.B. Williams	351*	0.8
	Birmingham, Northfield	69	D.W. Robinson	605*	0.9
	Birmingham, Stechford	74	S.C. Pegg	298*	0.7
	Bristol, North-West	98	W.E. Williams	227*	0.4
	Coventry, East	109	J. Hosey	841*	1.4
	Dagenham	119	G.C. Wake	982*	2.2
	Eccles	132	T.E. Keenan	643*	1.5
	Hayes and Harlington	153	P. Pink	372*	1.1
	Hornsey	158	Mrs. M. Morris	624*	1.4
	Huddersfield, East	160	Mrs. E. Beresford	308*	0.7
	Leeds, East	174	Mrs. J. Bellamy	513*	1.0

Communist Party of Great Britain

1970	Leeds, South-East	179	B. Scott	199*	1.1
(cont.)	Liverpool, Exchange	189	R. O'Hara	775*	4.2
	Luton	197	Dr. A.P.J. Chater	447*	1.0
	Manchester, Openshaw	205	B. Panter	552*	1.7
	Mitcham	211	S.E. French	638*	1.3
	Nottingham, North	223	J.H. Peck	741*	1.5
	Sheffield, Brightside	256	G. Ashberry	665*	2.0
	Sheffield, Park	261	C. Morton	637*	2.1
	Stockton-on-Tees	273	E. Jones	369*	0.9
	Stoke-on-Trent, South	276	S.J. Lomas	364*	1.1
	Swindon	283	Miss J. Gradwell	456*	1.0
	Walsall, North	292	D.J. Brayford	597*	1.2
	Wigan	305	J. Kay	672*	1.6
	Willesden, West	307	L.G. Burt	515*	1.6
	Wolverhampton, South-West	310	P.E. Carter	189*	0.5
	Huyton	423	J.I. Kenny	890*	1.2
	Mansfield	464	F.C. Westacott	628*	1.4
	Aberdare	543	Dr. A.T.M. Wilson	1,317*	3.5
	Rhondda, East	549	A.L. Jones	659*	2.3
	Rhondda, West	550	A. True	1,201*	4.8
	Swansea, East	551	W.R. Jones	563*	1.4
	Llanelli	559	R.E. Hitchon	603*	1.2
	Aberavon	564	Dr. J.T. Hart	1,102*	2.4
	Neath	568	H. Pearce	579*	1.5
	Pontypool	576	B. Wilkinson	435*	1.1
	Aberdeen, North	579	A.J. Ingram	521*	1.2
	Dundee, West	583	H. McLevy	809*	1.6
	Dunfermline Burghs	584	J. Neilson	462*	1.2
	Edinburgh, East	586	Mrs. I. Swan	413*	1.0
	Glasgow, Gorbals	597	J.R. Kay	376*	2.5
	Glasgow, Govan	598	T. Biggam	326*	1.5
	Glasgow, Provan	603	J. Jackson	601*	1.4
	Glasgow, Scotstoun	604	H.D. Boyd	846*	1.8
	Glasgow, Springburn	606	N. McLellan	423*	1.8
	Greenock	609	A.C. Murray	559*	1.6
	Dunbartonshire, East	627	J. Reid	1,656*	2.3
	Fife, West	630	A.D. MacMillan	855*	1.7
	Lanark	637	D. McDowall	1,273*	1.9
	Motherwell	638	J.W. Sneddon	1,829*	4.7
	West Lothian	653	C. Bett	459*	0.8
1972 (13/4)	Merthyr Tydfil	547	A.L. Jones	1,519*	4.7

1974 (F)	Barking, Dagenham	2	G.C. Wake	1,169*	2.4
	Brent, South	12	L.G. Burt	380*	0.9
	Camden, St. Pancras North	19	G. McLennan	466*	1.7
	Hackney, North and Stoke				
	Newington	37	M. Goldman	532*	1.6
	Islington, South and				
	Finsbury	57	Mrs. M. Betteridge	492*	1.8
	Merton, Mitcham and				
	Morden	69	S.E. French	507*	1.0
	Tower Hamlets, Stepney and				
	Poplar	85	K. Halpin	1,278*	3.6
	Wandsworth, Tooting	92	R.E. Lewis	337*	0.9
	Birmingham, Northfield	109	D.W. Robinson	368*	0.7
	Bootle	123	R. Morris	586*	1.3
	Coventry, North-East	146	J. Hosey	838*	1.7
	Eccles	158	T.E. Keenan	404*	0.9
	Huddersfield, East	178	A.J. Drake	246*	0.6
	Leeds, South-East	191	W.H. Innes	405*	1.2
	Liverpool, Scotland				
	Exchange	201	R. O'Hara	505*	2.5
	Manchester, Openshaw	213	P. Widdall	312*	1.0
	Nottingham, North	228	J.H. Peck	754*	1.3
	Sheffield, Brightside	255	Miss V.A. Gill	513*	1.3
	Sheffield, Park	259	C. Morton	521*	1.1
	Stoke-on-Trent, South	272	S.J. Lomas	481*	0.9
	Teesside, Stockton	280	E. Jones	791*	1.2
	Walsall, North	290	J. Richards	819*	1.6
	Mansfield	443	F.C. Westacott	675*	1.3
	Aberdare	517	Dr. A.T.M. Wilson	1,038*	2.6
	Merthyr Tydfil	522	A.L. Jones	369*	1.2
	Rhondda	524	A. True	1,374*	2.6
	Swansea, East	525	W.R. Jones	507*	1.2
	Llanelli	533	R.E. Hitchon	507*	1.0
	Pontypool	550	G.R. Williams	498*	1.2
	Dundee, West	557	H. McLevy	675*	1.3
	Edinburgh, East	559	Mrs. I. Swan	274*	0.6
	Glasgow, Garscadden	568	S. Barr	635*	1.6
	Glasgow, Pollok	573	T. Biggam	377*	0.8
	Glasgow, Provan	574	J. Jackson	749*	2.0
	Glasgow, Queen's Park	575	J.R. Kay	372*	1.3
	Glasgow, Springburn	577	N. McLellan	478*	1.4
	Greenock and Port Glasgow	578	A.C. Murray	483*	1.1

Communist Party of Great Britain

1974 (F)	Motherwell and Wishaw	579	J.W. Sneddon	1,066*	2.7
(cont.)	Dunbartonshire, Central	596	J. Reid	5,928	14.6
	Fife, Central	599	A. Maxwell	2,019*	4.4
	Bothwell	607	D. Bolton	562*	1.2
	East Kilbride	608	D. McDowall	693*	1.3
	Clackmannan and East Stirlingshire	621	G. Bolton	322*	0.6
	West Lothian	623	C. Bett	438*	0.7
1974 (O)	Barking, Dagenham	2	G.C. Wake	569*	1.3
	Hackney, North and Stoke Newington	37	M. Goldman	418*	1.5
	Islington, South and Finsbury	57	Mrs. M. Betteridge	512*	2.2
	Merton, Mitcham and Morden	69	S.E. French	281*	0.6
	Tower Hamlets, Stepney and Poplar	85	K. Halpin	617*	2.0
	Wandsworth, Tooting	92	R.E. Lewis	268*	0.8
	Birmingham, Northfield	109	D.W. Robinson	180*	0.3
	Bootle	123	R. Morris	516*	1.2
	Coventry, North-East	146	J. Hosey	309*	0.7
	Eccles	158	T.E. Keenan	348*	0.8
	Leeds, South-East	191	W.H. Innes	317*	1.1
	Liverpool, Scotland Exchange	201	R. O'Hara	556*	3.0
	Manchester, Openshaw	213	P. Widdall	300*	1.1
	Nottingham, North	228	J.H. Peck	525*	1.0
	Sheffield, Park	259	G. Ashberry	403*	1.0
	Walsall, North	290	J. Richards	465*	1.0
	Mansfield	443	F.C. Westacott	448*	0.9
	Aberdare	517	Dr. A.T.M. Wilson	1,028*	2.7
	Merthyr Tydfil	522	T.W. Roberts	509*	1.7
	Rhondda	524	A. True	1,404*	2.8
	Dundee, West	557	H. McLevy	381*	0.8
	Edinburgh, East	559	Mrs. I. Swan	213*	0.5
	Glasgow, Provan	574	J. Jackson	503*	1.4
	Glasgow, Queen's Park	575	J.R. Kay	354*	1.4
	Glasgow, Springburn	577	N. McLellan	352*	1.1
	Motherwell and Wishaw	579	J.W. Sneddon	946*	2.4
	Dunbartonshire, Central	596	J. Reid	3,417*	8.7
	Fife, Central	599	A. Maxwell	1,040*	2.4
	West Lothian	623	C. Bett	247*	0.4

[1] Until 1924 it was possible for members of the Communist Party to secure adoption and endorsement as official Labour Party candidates. The following is a summary of these candidates who are not included in the above table:—

| 1922: | S. Saklatavala (Battersea, North) polled 11,311 votes and was elected. |

M.P. Price (Gloucester) polled 7,871 votes and was defeated. It appears that he was not an actual member of the Communist Party at this election but "The Communist" of November 25, 1922, described him as 'sympathetic'.

| 1923 | W. Paul (Manchester, Rusholme) polled 5,366 votes and was defeated. |

M.P. Price (Gloucester) polled 8,127 votes and was defeated.

S. Saklatvala (Battersea, North) polled 12,341 votes and was defeated.

J.J. Vaughan (Bethnal Green, South-West) polled 5,251 votes and was defeated.

Miss E.C. Wilkinson (Ashton-under-Lyne) polled 6,208 votes and was defeated.

CO-OPERATIVE PARTY

Formed, as the Central Co-operative Parliamentary Representation Committee, at a
National Emergency Conference of the Co-operative Union held in London in October
1917. The 1918 Co-operative Congress upgraded the status of the committee (it had
originally been a sub committee of the Joint Parliamentary Committee of the Co-operative
Union) and the word 'National' was substituted for 'Central'. The 1919 Congress approved
a change of name to Co-operative Party. From after the General Election of 1918 all
Co-operative Party candidates were approved by the Labour Party and since 1927 various
electoral agreements have existed between the two parties.

Policy: The original aims of the party were to obtain direct representation of
Co-operators in Parliament; the formation of a Government based on
democratic principles; the establishment of a Co-operative Commonwealth
in which the incentive in industry would be production for use and not
for profit, allied to common ownership. Since 1927 when the party has
had electoral agreements with the Labour Party its policy has been broadly
that of the Labour Party with special emphasis on the furtherance of
consumers' interests.

Sources: Carbery, Thomas F., *Consumers in Politics: A History and General Review
of the Co-operative Party.* 1969.
Smith, Barbara and Ostergaard, Geoffrey, *Constitutional Relations between
the Labour and Co-operative Parties: An Historical Review.* 1960
Co-operative Congress Reports, 1917—
Co-operative News, 1917—
Scottish Co-operator, 1917—

Elections:

1918 (31/1)	Prestwich	312	H.J. May	2,832	24.9
1918	Birmingham, King's Norton	80	T. Hackett	4,917	30.4
	Birmingham, Sparkbrook	83	F. Spires	3,014	15.5
	Bradford, South	96	W. Hirst	8,291	30.9
	Leeds, Central	152	J. Smith	2,146	13.2
	Sheffield, Hillsborough	228	A. Lockwood	4,050	26.6
	Mossley	385	W.H. Brown	5,227	24.4
	Kettering	420	†A.E. Waterson[1]	10,299	45.7
	Paisley	578	J.M. Biggar	7,436	33.5
	Kilmarnock	585	P. Malcolm	6,652	32.9
	Clackmannan and Eastern Stirlingshire	616	H.J. May	5,753	32.8

After 1918 all Co-operative Party candidates were either
approved or endorsed by the Labour Party.

[1] Joined the Parliamentary Labour Party in February 1919.

DEMOCRATIC PARTY [1]

Formed in 1942 by Major Norman Leith-Hay-Clark. Re-named Independent Democratic Party shortly after the General Election of 1945. In 1961 the party was still in existence but by then it concerned itself with investigating cases of personal hardship and was no longer politically active.

Policy: Free-enterprise and efficient business organisation; profit-sharing for workers; simplified taxation; the limitation of excessive individual incomes.

Sources: *The Policy of the Democratic Party.* (Pamphlet), 1944

Elections:

1945					
Westminster, Abbey	58	N. Leith-Hay-Clark	326*	1.9	
Portsmouth, Central	207	W.R.C. Foster	561*	2.1	
Portsmouth, North	208	J.E.V. Keast	388*	1.3	
Maidstone	371	G. Murray	416*	1.0	
Chichester	467	P.T. Carter	118*	0.2	

DEMOCRATIC PARTY [2]

Formed by Desmond Donnelly in May 1969. In April 1971 Donnelly joined the Conservative Party and announced that he had severed his connections with the Democratic Party which appears to have subsequently disbanded.

Policy:	Anti-socialist.
Sources:	*The Times,* 1969—70
Secessions:	D.L. Donnelly (Pembrokeshire) who had been elected at the General Election of 1966 as a Labour MP, resigned the Labour whip in January 1968. In March 1968 he was expelled from the Labour Party and one month later the Pembrokeshire Constituency Labour Party was disaffiliated. He remained an Independent Labour MP until the formation of the Democratic Party.

Elections:

1969 (30/10)	Newcastle-under-Lyme	213	D. Parker	1,699*	3.6
1969 (4/12)	Louth	444	Sir G.P.M. FitzGerald, Bt.	1,225*	4.4
1970	Newcastle-under-Lyme	213	Dr. P.H. Boyle	1,194*	2.6
	Reading	241	A. Boothroyd	867*	1.8
	Devon, North	354	B.G. Morris	175*	0.4
	Huyton	423	J.W.G. Sparrow	1,232*	1.7
	Pembrokeshire	578	D.L. Donnelly	11,824	21.5

EMPIRE FREE TRADE CRUSADE

Launched by Lord Beaverbrook in the *Daily Express* during the summer of 1929. In December 1929 the Crusade organisers asked for subscriptions and enrolled individual members. It ceased activities following the General Election of 1931.

Policy: Empire free trade.

Sources: *Daily Express*, 1929–31

Elections:

1930 (30/10)	Paddington, South	38	†E.A. Taylor[1]	11,209	37.4
1931 (19/2)	Islington, East	25	A.C. Critchley[2]	8,314	27.2

[1] At the General Election of 1931 Taylor was adopted for the constituency as the official Conservative candidate and was re-elected.

[2] Joint candidate of the Empire Free Trade Crusade and the United Empire Party.

FELLOWSHIP PARTY

Formed in London, June 1955. The party arose as a result of opposition to the British manufacture of the hydrogen bomb and two of its founders (John Loverseed and Eric Fenner) had contested the General Election of 1955 as anti-hydrogen bomb candidates.

Policy: Pacifism.

Sources: *Progress*, 1956—

Elections:

1959	Woolwich, West	46	R.S. Mallone	1,189*	2.6
1964	Woolwich, West	46	R.S. Mallone	1,112*	2.5
1966	Woolwich, West	46	R.S. Mallone	906*	2.1
1969 (26/6)	Birmingham, Ladywood	68	A.J.W. Haigh	34*	0.4
1971 (8/7)	Greenwich	14	R.S. Mallone	792*	3.6

HIGHLAND LAND LEAGUE

Formed at a meeting in Glasgow in August 1909 (an earlier body of the same name had been formed in 1887 as the result of a merger between the Highland Land Law Reform Association (Edinburgh) and the Highland and Land Law Reform Association (London) but had ceased activities during the mid 1890s) and in August 1918 the League announced that it had decided to 'link-up with the Labour Party'. The following month, the annual conference of the Labour Party (Scottish Advisory Council) approved an agreement with the League which provided for co-operation in selecting candidates and raising funds. The candidates put forward by the League at the General Election of 1918 were all members of the Labour Party and the 1919 annual report of the party's Scottish Advisory Council's executive committee reported that the candidates had received official endorsement by the Labour Party in London. This statement appears to be incorrect for the official list of Labour Party candidates in 1918 does not include the names of any of the League's nominees. The League appears to have ceased activities in the early 1920s.

Policy:	To being about the restoration of the people to the soil by (a) the utilisation of fertile lands now used as deer forests and other sporting tracts with adequate common pasture lands; (b) the abolition of plural farmers and the replacing of them by small farmers and crofters and (c) the resumption of the ownership and control of the land by the state.
	The League also pledged itself to defend crofters and cottars who might be threatened with eviction or subjected to oppressive measures by landlords or their agents.
	The League favoured home rule for Scotland.

Sources: Labour Party (Scottish Advisory Council) Annual Reports, 1918—19
Glasgow Herald, 1909—18
Scotsman, 1909—18
Scottish Review, Vol. 41, pp. 544—7

Elections:

1918	Argyll	583	L.M. Weir	2,733	18.6
	Inverness	596	G.J. Bruce	2,930	26.8
	Ross and Cromarty	597	H. Munro	2,238	21.1
	Western Isles	598	H. McCowan	809*	10.2

INDEPENDENT DEMOCRATIC ALLIANCE

Formed in London, April 1973, as the result of the amalgamation of the All Party Alliance (led by John Creasey) and The Organisation (led by Colin Campion).

Policy: To secure, support and sustain democratic Government controlled by the people.

Sources: None traced.

Elections:

1974 (F)	Batley and Morley	101	G. Jarratt	828*	1.7
	Bradford, West	128	R.O. Herbert	200*	0.4
	Brighouse and Spenborough	129	Mrs. S.V. Milner	169*	0.3
	Horncastle	426	E.P. Iszatt	367*	0.9
	Eye	466	A.W.G. Kingham	220*	0.4
	Shipley	514	C.G. Campion	192*	0.4

In addition to those listed above, the following candidates ran as Independents but were associated with or members of the IDA.

	Blackpool, South	118	E. Mills[1]	229*	0.5
	Stroud	372	J.S. Churchill[2]	470*	0.8
	Worcestershire, South	495	G. Hunt[2]	850*	1.4

[1] Ran as a National Independent.
[2] Ran as an Independent Conservative.

INDEPENDENT LABOUR PARTY

Formed in January 1893 at a conference in Bradford attended by delegates from various Socialist organisations who sought to create a united party. The ILP was affiliated to the Labour Party from the latter's formation in February 1900 (as the Labour Representation Committee) until August 1932 when they disaffiliated.

Policy: Socialism.

Sources: Bealey, F. & Pelling, H., *Labour and Politics 1900–1906*. 1958
Cole, G.D.H., *British Working Class Politics 1832–1914*. 1941
Cole, G.D.H., *A History of the Labour Party from 1914*. 1948
Dowse, R.E., *Left in the Centre: The Independent Labour Party 1893–1940*. 1966
Marwick, A.J., *The Independent Labour Party 1918–1932*. B. Litt. Thesis, Oxford, 1960
Labour Leader, 1893–1922
New Leader, 1922–1949
Socialist Leader, 1949–

Secessions: J.K. Hardie (West Ham, South) who had been elected as an Independent Labour MP at the General Election of 1892, joined the ILP when it was founded.
G. Buchanan (Glasgow, Gorbals) and D. Kirkwood (Dumbarton Burghs) who had been elected at the General Election of 1931 as unendorsed Labour MPs (they were members of the ILP but not official candidates of that party) joined the ILP parliamentary group upon election. Kirkwood was expelled from the party in August 1932 and joined the Labour Party.

Elections:

1893 (9/2)	Halifax	110	J. Lister	3,028	25.4
1894 (5/7)	Sheffield, Attercliffe	172	F.S. Smith	1,249	13.5
1894 (29/8)	Leicester	128	J. Burgess	4,402	15.7
1895	Fulham	14	W. Parnell	196	2.1
	Ashton-under-Lyne	59	J. Sexton	415	6.4
	Barrow-in-Furness	61	P.F. Curran	414	6.9
	Bolton [2]	73	F. Brocklehurst	2,694	9.8
	Bradford, West	77	B. Tillett	2,264	23.4
	Bristol, East	79	S.G. Hobson	1,874	31.2
	Dewsbury	99	E.R. Hartley	1,080	10.5
	Halifax [2]	110	J. Lister	3,818	20.5
	Huddersfield	115	H.R. Smart	1,594	11.2
	Kingston upon Hull, West	122	T. McCarthy	1,400	17.4
	Leeds, South	126	A. Shaw	622	6.4
	Leicester [2]	128	J. Burgess	4,009	13.7

Independent Labour Party

1895	Manchester, North-East	142	J. Johnston	546	6.6
(cont.)	Newcastle upon Tyne [2]	149	F.P. Hammill	2,302	4.6
	Preston [2]	162	J. Tattersall	4,781	22.4
	Rochdale	164	G.N. Barnes	1,251	12.0
	Southampton [2]	178	J.R. Macdonald	867	4.0
	West Ham, South	195	J.K. Hardie	3,975	45.6
	Hyde	219	G.S. Christie	448	5.0
	Gorton	303	Dr. R.M. Pankhurst	4,261	42.1
	Colne Valley	419	T. Mann	1,245	13.4
	Dundee [2]	473	J. Macdonald	1,313	5.0
	Glasgow, Blackfriars and Hutchesontown	480	J.S. Maxwell	448	7.1
	Glasgow, Bridgeton	481	Prof. J.R. Watson	609	9.4
	Glasgow, Camlachie	482	R. Smillie	696	10.9
	Glasgow, St. Rollox	485	J.E. Woolacott	405	4.4
	Glasgow, Tradeston	486	F.S. Smith	368	5.8
	Govan	520	A. Haddow	430	4.9
1896 (1/5)	Aberdeen, North	469	T. Mann	2,479	46.0
1896 (10/11)	Bradford, East	76	J.K. Hardie	1,953	17.1
1897 (3/3)	Halifax	110	T. Mann	2,000	15.5
1897 (28/10)	Barnsley	418	P.F. Curran	1,091	9.7

From the formation of the Labour Representation Committee in 1900 until the ILP disaffiliated in August 1932, ILP nominees were normally endorsed as official Labour candidates by the LRC (in Scotland by the Scottish Workers' Representation Committee/ Scottish Labour Party) and after 1906 by the Labour Party.

The following candidates did not however receive official Labour endorsement and ran as candidates of the ILP only:

1912 (22/8)	Carmarthenshire, Eastern	452	Dr. J.H. Williams	1,089	10.3
1918 (26/4)	Keighley	424	W. Bland	2,349	32.5
1930 (28/11)	Renfrewshire, Eastern	613	T. Irwin	12,293	33.3
1931	Camberwell, Peckham	10	J. Beckett	11,217	33.5
	Wandsworth, Clapham	55	Miss H.A. Browning	7,317	23.0
	Bradford, East	94	Rt. Hon. F.W. Jowett	15,779	41.2
	Leyton, East	162	A.F. Brockway	10,433	37.6
	Liverpool, Kirkdale	170	E. Sandham	9,531	30.1
	Norwich [2]	197	Miss D. Jewson	26,537	19.7
	Stockport [2]	236	J.T. Abbot	15,591	11.3

	Camborne	294	Miss K.F. Spurrell	8,280	24.5
	Merthyr Tydfil, Merthyr	518	†R.C. Wallhead[1]	24,623	69.4
	Glasgow, Bridgeton	559	†J. Maxton	16,630	58.2
	Glasgow, Camlachie	560	Rev. C. Stephen	15,282	45.3
	Glasgow, Kelvingrove	566	J. Winning	12,415	36.6
	Glasgow, Shettleston	571	†J. McGovern	16,301	47.8
	Bute and Northern Ayrshire	584	A. Sloan	10,227	29.5
	Kilmarnock	585	J. Pollock	14,767	40.4
	Lanark	602	J. Gibson	11,815	36.4
	Lanarkshire, Northern	604	Miss J. Lee	19,691	44.7
	Perth	612	Mrs. H.E. Gault	3,705*	9.7
	Renfrewshire, Western	614	Mrs. J. Mann	10,203	31.5
1932 (9/2)	New Forest and Christchurch	349	Dr. C.A. Smith	5,135	18.0
1933 (2/11)	Kilmarnock	585	J. Pollock	7,575	20.9
1934 (14/5)	West Ham, Upton	261	A.F. Brockway	748*	3.5
1934 (5/6)	Merthyr Tydfil, Merthyr	518	Rev. C. Stephen	3,508*	9.8
1935	Bradford, East	94	Rt. Hon. F.W. Jowett	8,983	26.6
	Norwich [2]	197	A.F. Brockway	6,737*	5.5
	Camborne	294	Miss K.F. Spurrell	592*	1.9
	Whitehaven	300	T. Stephenson	1,004*	3.3
	Chorley	375	R. Edwards	1,365*	3.3
	Merthyr Tydfil, Merthyr	518	C. Stanfield	9,640	32.0
	Aberdeen, North	548	A.F. Macintosh	3,871*	11.1
	Glasgow, Bridgeton	559	†J. Maxton	17,691	64.9
	Glasgow, Camlachie	560	†Rev. C. Stephen	15,070	47.2
	Glasgow, Gorbals	563	†G. Buchanan[2]	22,860	75.0
	Glasgow, Govan	564	T. Taylor	4,959	16.0
	Glasgow, Shettleston	571	†J. McGovern	18,377	52.8
	Glasgow, Tradeston	573	J. Carmichael	3,423	13.2
	Kilmarnock	585	J. Pollock	3,582*	9.5
	Lanark	602	W. Carlin	2,583*	8.3
	Lanarkshire, Northern	604	Miss J. Lee	17,267	37.3
	Clackmannan and Eastern Stirlingshire	616	D.W. Gibson	1,573*	4.5
1939 (8/12)	Stretford	389	R. Edwards	4,424	15.1
1940 (9/5)	Renfrewshire, Eastern	613	Miss A. Maxton	8,206	19.3
1941 (15/10)	Lancaster	382	A.F. Brockway	5,418	19.5
1941 (11/12)	Edinburgh, Central	554	T. Taylor	1,950	29.0
1942 (13/4)	Cardiff, East	515	A.F. Brockway	3,311	24.8
1942 (28/4)	Glasgow, Cathcart	561	J. Carmichael	2,493	13.8
1943 (18/2)	Bristol, Central	98	J. McNair	830*	7.4
1943 (10/11)	Woolwich, West	61	W.T. Colyer	3,419	27.2

Independent Labour Party

Year	Constituency	No.	Candidate	Votes	%
1943 (14/12)	Acton	404	W.E. Padley	2,336	28.1
1944 (20/9)	Wolverhampton, Bilston	266	A. Eaton	9,344	49.1
1945 (17/5)	Newport	519	R. Edwards	13,722	45.5
1945	Bradford, East	94	W. Ballantine	5,195	14.8
	Wolverhampton, Bilston	266	A. Eaton	849*	1.8
	Glasgow, Bridgeton	559	†J. Maxton[3]	13,220	66.4
	Glasgow, Camlachie	560	†Rev. C. Stephen[4]	15,558	57.7
	Glasgow, Shettleston	571	†J. McGovern[5]	11,947	35.4
1946 (25/7)	Battersea, North	1	H. Dewar	240*	1.5
1946 (29/8)	Glasgow, Bridgeton	559	†J. Carmichael[6]	6,351	34.3
1947 (11/9)	Liverpool, Edge Hill	166	D.W. Gibson	154*	0.7
1948 (28/1)	Glasgow, Camlachie	560	Miss A. Maxton	1,622*	6.4
1950	Burnley	103	D. Carradice	295*	0.5
	Newcastle upon Tyne, Central	214	F.G. Barton	812*	2.1
	Glasgow, Bridgeton	592	R. Duncan	1,974*	5.8
	Glasgow, Shettleston	605	J.W. Graham	1,031*	2.5
1950 (25/10)	Glasgow, Scotstoun	604	D.W. Gibson	680*	1.9
1951 (5/4)	Ormskirk	430	F.G. Barton	686*	2.0
1951	Newcastle upon Tyne, Central	214	F.G. Barton	1,066*	2.7
	Glasgow, Bridgeton	592	R. Duncan	1,796*	5.4
	Glasgow, Shettleston	605	J.W. Graham	1,195*	2.8
1955	Bermondsey	4	H.S. Birkett	715*	2.5
	Glasgow, Bridgeton	592	G.W. Stone	2,619*	7.4
1957 (30/5)	East Ham, North	130	W.H. Christopher	458*	2.1
1958 (13/3)	Glasgow, Kelvingrove	600	W.C. Park	587*	2.8
1958 (15/5)	Islington, North	22	J. McKie	576*	3.0
1959	Walthamstow, East	294	W.H. Christopher	183*	0.5
	Glasgow, Kelvingrove	600	W.C. Park	740*	3.0
1961 (16/11)	Glasgow, Bridgeton	592	G.W. Stone	586*	3.1
1966	Leyton	186	W.R. Hanley	441*	0.9
1970	Halifax	147	A.J.W. Graham	847*	1.7

[1] Resigned from the ILP and joined the Labour Party, May 1933.
[2] Resigned from the ILP and joined the Labour Party, May 1939.
[3] Died July 1946.
[4] Resigned from the ILP and joined the Labour Party, October 1947.
[5] Resigned from the ILP and joined the Labour Party, March 1947.
[6] Resigned from the ILP and joined the Labour Party, November 1947.

INDEPENDENT NUCLEAR DISARMAMENT
ELECTION COMMITTEE

Formed in April 1962 by a number of members of the Campaign for Nuclear Disarmament including Miss Pat Attowsmith and Miss Vanessa Redgrave. The Committee appears to have been dissolved after the General Election of 1964.

Policy: Unilateral nuclear disarmament.

Sources: Duff, Peggy, *Left, Left, Left.* 1971
Sanity, 1961–

Elections:

1964	Bromley	102	A.J.W. Haigh	461*	1.2
	Twickenham	286	M.H. Craft	1,073*	1.9

INDEPENDENT PARLIAMENTARY GROUP

The group, led by Horatio Bottomley, M.P. (Hackney, South), emerged during 1920. It probably disbanded shortly after Bottomley's imprisionment for fraud in May 1922.

Policy: Payment of all war indemnities and repatriations to be sternly enforced; British supremacy to be maintained unfettered by Leagues of Nations; public expenditure to be cut down and the introduction of business principles into the Government.

Sources: Symons, Julian, *Horatio Bottomley*. 1955
     John Bull, 1920–21

Secessions: A.C.T. Beck (Saffron Walden) who had been elected as a Coalition Liberal at the General Election of 1918 joined the group in August 1921.
C.W. Lowther (Cumberland, Northern) and C.W.H. Lowther (Lonsdale) who had been elected at the General Election of 1918 as Coalition Conservatives joined the group in January and July 1921 respectively.
Beck did not seek re-election at the General Election of 1922. C.W. Lowther obtained adoption as Conservative candidate for Wallsend but was defeated.
C.W.H. Lowther obtained adoption as Conservative candidate for Carlisle but was defeated.

Elections:

Bottomley, later assisted by members of his group,
supported the following candidates at by-elections:

1920 (7/2)	The Wrekin	436	†C.F. Palmer[1] (Ind)	9,267	40.7
1920 (27/3)	Dartford	366	R.V.K. Applin (Nat P)	2,952*	10.9
1920 (27/3)	Stockport [2]	236	A.A.G. Kindell (Ind)	5,644*	6.3
			J.J. Terrett (Ind)	5,443*	6.1
1920 (20/11)	The Wrekin	436	†Sir C.V.F. Townshend[2] (Ind)	14,565	57.9
1921 (12/1)	Dover	367	†Sir T.A. Polson[3] (Ind)	13,947	56.3
1921 (16/6)	Hertford	356	†M.F. Sueter[4] (Ind)	12,329	68.9
1921 (25/8)	Westminster, Abbey	58	†J.S. Nicholson[5] (C)	6,204	43.6

[1] Died October 1920.

[2] Joined the Conservative Party in February 1922.

[3] Joined the Anti-Waste League when it was formed shortly after his election but Bottomley continued to claim him as a member of his group.

[4] Joint candidate of the group and the Anti-Waste League.

[5] Although supported by the group it appears that Nicholson never actually joined it.

INTERNATIONAL MARXIST GROUP

Formed (as the British Section of the Fourth International) in November 1966 by a number of former members of the Communist Party of Great Britain.

Policy: Communism (Trotskyist).

Sources: *The Week*, 1965–67
Black Dwarf, 1968–70
Red Mole, 1970–73
Red Weekly, 1973–

Elections:

1974 (F)	Newham, North-East	71	J.M. Ross	202*	0.4
	Sheffield, Attercliffe	254	T. Ali	424*	0.9
	Glasgow, Queen's Park	575	R.M. Purdie	90*	0.3

IRISH CIVIL RIGHTS ASSOCIATION

Formed in Dublin, December 1972.

Policy: Phased withdrawal of British troops from Ulster; end of internment and an amnesty for political prisoners.

Sources: *Irish Post*, 1973—
*Irish People, 1973—

Elections:

1974 (O)[1]	Brent, East	10	J. Curran	382*	1.0
	Camden, Hampstead	17	Mrs. M.F.T. Maguire	146*	0.3
	City of Westminster, Paddington	21	J.S. Allman	135*	0.4
	Hammersmith, North	40	J.P. McFadden	633*	1.9
	Birmingham, Sparkbrook	113	J. Molloy	548*	1.8
	Luton, East	206	L.T. Byrne	299*	0.8
	Manchester, Moss Side	212	N. Boyle	238*	0.7

[1] The British branch of the Association was expelled by the ICRA executive on October 2, 1974, for its decision to put forward parliamentary candidates.

IRISH NATIONALIST MOVEMENT

The Irish nationalist movement in Great Britain was represented by branches of the principal nationalist bodies including the National League (formed in October 1882 by Charles Stewart Parnell) and the United Irish League (formed in 1898 by William O'Brien).

Policy: Irish nationalism.

Sources: Lyons, F.S.L., *The Irish Parliamentary Party, 1890–1910*. 1951
Norman, Edward, *A History of Modern Ireland*. 1971
O'Connor, T.P., *Memoirs of an Old Parliamentarian*. 1929

Elections:

1885	Liverpool, Kirkdale	134	J.E. Redmond	765	12.5
	Liverpool, Scotland	135	†T.P. O'Connor	2,724	64.9
1886	Liverpool, Scotland	135	†T.P. O'Connor	2,911	67.0
1892	Liverpool, Scotland	135	†T.P. O'Connor	2,537	65.3
1895	Liverpool, Scotland	135	†T.P. O'Connor	2,089	59.0
1900	Liverpool, Scotland	135	†T.P. O'Connor	2,044	57.9
1906	Liverpool, Scotland	135	†T.P. O'Connor	2,808	71.5
1910 (J)	Liverpool, Scotland	135	†T.P. O'Connor	2,943	79.1
1910 (D)	Liverpool, Scotland	135	†T.P. O'Connor	2,458	78.1
1918	Liverpool, Exchange	168	A. Harford	8,225	44.4
	Liverpool, Scotland	171	†T.P. O'Connor	unopposed	
1922	Liverpool, Exchange	168	J. Devlin	12,614	44.6
	Liverpool, Scotland	171	†T.P. O'Connor	unopposed	
1923	Liverpool, Exchange	168	W. Grogan	10,322	49.5
	Liverpool, Scotland	171	†T.P. O'Connor	unopposed	
1924	Liverpool, Scotland	171	†Rt. Hon. T.P. O'Connor	unopposed	
1929	Liverpool, Scotland	171	†Rt. Hon. T.P. O'Connor[1]	unopposed	

[1] Died, November, 1929

LABOUR INDEPENDENT GROUP

The formation of the group was announced in June 1949. It consisted of four MPs who had been expelled from the Labour Party for persistent opposition to official party policy, especially in the sphere of foreign affairs.

The group disbanded as the result of the defeat of all its members at the General Election of 1950.

Policy: Socialism.

Sources: Pritt, D.N., *Autobiography of D.N. Pritt. Part 2. Brasshats and Bureaucrats.* 1966.
The Times, 1949–50

Secessions: D.N. Pritt (Hammersmith, North) who had been elected at the General Election of 1945 as an Independent Labour MP (he had been expelled from the Labour Party in March 1940) became chairman of the group when it was formed.

J.F.F. Platts-Mills (Finsbury), L.J. Solley (Thurrock) and K. Zilliacus (Gateshead) who had been elected at the General Election of 1945 as Labour MPs but who had been expelled from the party between 1948 and 1949 (Platts-Mills in April 1948; Solley and Zilliacus in May 1949) joined the group when it was formed.

H.L. Hutchinson (Manchester, Rusholme) who had been elected at the General Election of 1945 as a Labour MP was expelled from the party in July 1949 and joined the group.

Elections:

1950					
Hammersmith, North	17	D.N. Pritt	8,457	25.2
Shoreditch and Finsbury	37	J.F.F. Platts-Mills	7,602	18.0
Gateshead, East	141	K. Zilliacus	5,001	14.8
Walthamstow, West	295	H.L. Hutchinson	704*	2.0
Thurrock	381	L.J. Solley	4,250*	9.8

LEAGUE OF EMPIRE LOYALISTS

Formed by A.K. Chesterton, April 1954. Merged in the National Front (q.v.) when it was formed in March 1967.

Policy: British nationalism.

Sources: *Candour*, 1954–62

Elections:

1957 (14/2)	Lewisham, North	29	Miss L.M.C. Greene	1,487*	4.0
1964	Wandsworth, Streatham	44	W.A. Brooks	497*	1.3
	Petersfield	391	Miss R.M. de Bounevialle	292*	0.7
	Fife, East	629	Miss L.M.C. Greene	257*	0.7

LIVERPOOL PROTESTANT PARTY

Formed by the Rev. George Wise in Liverpool, probably about 1903. The party is still active in contesting local government elections in Liverpool.

Policy: Protestantism.

Sources: *Protestant Standard* 1889–1916
                 Protestant Times, 1934–

Elections:

1931	Liverpool, Kirkdale	170	Rev. H.D. Longbottom	7,834	24.7
1935	Liverpool, Kirkdale	170	Rev. H.D. Longbottom	6,677	24.5
1945	Liverpool, Kirkdale	170	Rev. H.D. Longbottom	2,601	13.2

MEBYON KERNOW

Formed in 1951. The title of the party translates from the Cornish as 'Sons of Cornwall'.

Policy: To maintain the Celtic character of Cornwall and its right to self-government in domestic affairs.

Sources: *Cornish Nation, ? —*

Elections:

1970	Falmouth and Camborne	339	R.G. Jenkin	960*	2.0
1974 (F)	Truro	333	Dr. J.C.A. Whetter	850*	1.5
1974 (O)	Truro	333	Dr. J.C.A. Whetter	384*	0.7

MUDIAD GWERINIAETHOL CYMRU
(Welsh Republican Movement)

Formed in 1949 by a group of former members of Plaid Cymru. The movement was reported to be still active in 1966.

Policy: The creation of a Welsh socialist republic.

Sources: *Welsh Republican*, 1950—57

Elections:

| 1950 | Ogmore | 569 | I. Davies | 613* | 1.3 |

NATIONAL DEMOCRATIC AND LABOUR PARTY

Formed, as the Socialist National Defence Committee, April 1915. Renamed British Workers' National League, March 1916. The word 'National' was dropped from the title in March 1917 and in May 1918 the name was once again changed, this time to the National Democratic and Labour Party. In December 1921 the NDP reverted to its former title of British Workers' League and became purely a patriotic propaganda pressure group. In the autumn of 1925 it again changed its name (this time to the Empire Citizens' League) and after September 1927 its journal *Empire Citizen* ceased publication and the League probably disbanded shortly afterwards.

Policy: Support of the Coalition Government and the war effort. Broadly socialist in outlook and claimed to represent the 'patriotic working-class'. The party was bitterly opposed to the pacifist elements within the Labour Party.

Sources: Douglas, Roy, *The National Democratic Party and The British Workers' League. Historical Journal,* Vol. XV, 3 (1972), pp. 533—552
          British Citizen and Empire Worker, 1916—21
          Empire Citizen, 1921—27

Elections:

1918				
Accrington	62	W. Hammond	738*	2.5
Birmingham, Duddeston	76	†E. Hallas[1]	8,796	79.4
Bradford, East	94	†C.E. Loseby	9,390	41.1
Derby [2]	117	H.M. Smith	13,012	19.6
East Ham, South	124	†A.C. Edwards	7,972	42.8
Leicester, West	160	†J.F. Green	20,570	76.4
Morpeth	189	T.M. Allison	511*	2.3
Rochdale	213	J.J. Terrett	2,358*	7.8
Rotherham	218	E.S. Bardsley	564*	2.2
Stoke-on-Trent, Hanley	239	†J.A. Seddon	8,032	40.4
Tottenham, South	244	A.E. Harvey	1,916*	12.3
Wallsend	249	†M.T. Simm	10,246	50.9
Walthamstow, West	252	†C. Jesson	7,330	51.6
Wolverhampton, East	267	Rev. J.A. Shaw	7,138	48.2
Consett	325	R. Gee	7,283	32.9
Houghton-le-Spring	327	J. Lindsley	6,185	30.7
Broxtowe	427	H.H. Whaite	4,374	21.6
Mansfield	428	G.W.S. Jarrett	6,678	32.6
Nuneaton	471	W. Dyson	1,101*	4.5
Stourbridge	486	F.V. Fisher	6,690	28.8
Don Valley	497	†J. Walton	6,095	46.2
Rother Valley	506	E.G. Bearcroft	4,894	27.2

National Democratic and Labour Party

1918	Merthyr Tydfil, Aberdare	517	†C.B. Stanton	22,824	78.6
(cont.)	Dumbarton Burghs	551	†J. Taylor	11,734	52.6
	Edinburgh, East	555	A.E. Balfour	5,136	37.8
	Paisley	578	J. Taylor	7,201	32.5
	Hamilton	601	D. Gilmour	4,297	25.9
1919 (13/11)	Chester-le-Street	324	D. Gilmour	5,313	22.9
1920 (3/6)	Louth	403	C.H. Turnor[3]	7,354	42.7

At the General Election of 1922, the nine National Democratic and Labour Party MPs sought election under the auspices of the National Liberal organisation which had been formed by Lloyd George. All were defeated.

[1] Joined the Labour Party, October 1919. Did not seek re-election in 1922.

[2] There is some doubt as to whether or not Taylor should be included among the party's MPs. He was a Liberal supporter of the Coalition and was adopted by the local Liberal Association and supported by the NDP. It is unlikely that Taylor ever considered himself as other than a Coalition Liberal although the NDP did claim him as one of their MPs.

[3] Turnor, a member of the NDP, was adopted by the local Conservative Association and appears to have run as a Conservative rather than an NDP candidate. However, in a letter from W. Dudley Ward (a Coalition Liberal Whip) to Lloyd George on May 14, 1920 (Lloyd George papers F/22/1/35) Ward clearly states that Turnor was in fact an NDP candidate.

NATIONAL DEMOCRATIC PARTY

Formed by Dr. David R.M. Brown in January 1963.

Policy: British nationalism.

Sources: *Penny Post*, 1968—

Elections:

1964	Ipswich	164	Dr. D.R.M. Brown	349*	0.6
1966	Ipswich	164	Dr. D.R.M. Brown	769*	1.3
1970	Birmingham, Stechford	74	D. Hardy	1,438*	3.6
	Ipswich	164	Dr. D.R.M. Brown	2,322*	3.7
	Leicester, North-West	182	R.E. Welford	935*	2.5
	Southampton, Itchen	264	E.N.I. Bray	9,581	21.9
1971 (27/5)	Southampton, Itchen	264	E.N.I. Bray	3,090*	7.6
1974 (F)	Ipswich	181	Dr. D.R.M. Brown	1,161*	1.6

NATIONAL FARMERS' UNION OF ENGLAND AND WALES

Formed in London, December 1908. In 1909 the Union set up a Parliamentary Fund and a Central Parliamentary Committee with the object of supporting candidates nominated by county branches.

Policy: To protect the interests of farmers.

Sources: Self, P. and Storing, H., *The State and the Farmer.* 1962
                The National Farmers' Year Book and Annual Report, 1909–
                Parliamentary Bulletin, 1919–22
                N.F.U. Record, 1922–48
                British Farmer, 1948–

Elections:

1918 (4/5)	Ross	280	T. Preece[1]	1,784	35.4
1918	Barnard Castle	321	O. Monkhouse	1,274*	10.0
	Leominster	353	E.W. Langford	2,870	17.4
	Hertford	356	E.B. Barnard[2]	7,158	38.8
	Ormskirk	387	S. Hurst	4,989*	28.3
	Norfolk, Eastern	414	W.B. Taylor	1,926*	12.3
	Richmond (Yorks.)	491	W. Parlour	4,907	33.2
1922[3]	Rutland and Stamford	399	E. Clark	4,471	20.3
	Howdenshire	489	H.J. Winn	7,021	39.5
	Carmarthen	528	D. Johns	4,775	15.9

At the 1923 General Election the NFU sponsored four Conservative candidates, three of whom were elected; in 1924 and 1935 they sponsored two Conservatives at each election and all were successful. Sponsorship of candidates ceased after 1935.

[1] The nominee of the local branch of the NFU.

[2] Also the nominee of the National Party, (q.v.).

[3] In addition to the three candidates listed, the NFU also sponsored four Conservative candidates (at Leominster, Ormskirk, Stone and Wells) all of whom were elected.

NATIONAL FEDERATION OF DISCHARGED AND
DEMOBILIZED SAILORS AND SOLDIERS

Formed in April 1917. An ex-service organisation which merged with the British Legion when the latter was founded in 1921.

Policy: Welfare of ex-servicemen.

Sources: Wootton, Graham, *The Official History of the British Legion.* 1956
Wootton, Graham, *The Politics of Influence.* 1963
*D.S.S. Bulletin, 1919–21

Elections:

1917 (28/6)	Liverpool, Abercromby	130	F.B. Hughes	794	26.3
1918	Southwark, North	47	J.J. Gebbett	573*	6.3
	Ashton-under-Lyne	64	T.F. Lister	7,334	41.7
	Birmingham, Aston	74	J.H. Dooley	1,561*	9.8
	Kingston upon Hull, South-				
	West	150	A.E. Shakesby	695*	4.3
	Nottingham, East	199	J.N.D. Brookes	2,166	14.9

In addition to the above candidates who had been approved by the National Executive Committee of the Federation, the following independent candidates were either sponsored or supported by local NFDSS branches:

Battersea, South	2	J.E.P. Jenkin	1,657*	7.2
Bermondsey, West	4	H.T.A. Becker	1,294*	12.3
Bethnal Green, South-West	6	E. Thurtle	1,941	23.9
Deptford	13	F.A. Rumsey	2,106*	8.1
Fulham, West	16	W.J. Allen	995*	5.3
Islington, West	28	E.M. Taylor	1,105*	10.0
Lambeth, Brixton	31	S. Kelley	3,641	22.6
Lambeth, Norwood	34	H. Bignold	6,665	34.2
Paddington, North	37	E.P.J. Barry	3,571	20.7
Wandsworth, Clapham	55	H.H. Beamish	3,070	18.9
Birmingham, Handsworth	79	N. Tiptaft	4,697	22.1
Coventry	109	A.C. Bannington	3,806*	9.8
Great Yarmouth	130	W.H. Dawson[1]	125*	0.9
Grimsby	131	H.J.F. Crosby	1,260*	4.7
Leeds, Central	152	E. Terry[2]	2,634	16.2
Leeds, South	155	J.A. Brook[2]	1,377*	7.9
Leeds, West	157	J.H. Chapman[2]	1,138*	5.6
Liverpool, Everton	167	A.W. Brooksbank	5,779	47.6
Manchester, Hulme	181	G. Milner	729*	3.6

National Federation of Discharged and Demobilized Sailors and Soldiers

1918	Morpeth	189	G.D. Newton	2,729*	12.2
(cont.)	Newcastle upon Tyne, East	193	J.W. Thompson[3]	1,079*	7.2
	Tottenham, South	244	A.E. Jay	1,295*	8.3
	Wallasey	248	T.D. Owen	3,407	12.9
	Hitchin	357	G. Humm	722*	4.5
	Spelthorne	410	A.W. Leonard	1,143*	7.2
	Aberavon	533	T.G. Jones[4]	324*	1.5

[1] Dawson's candidature had at first been approved by the National Executive of the Federation but during the campaign they repudiated him.

[2] Also supported by the local branches of the other ex-service organisations — Comrades of the Great War and the National Association of Discharged Sailors and Soldiers.

[3] Thompson's candidature had at first been supported by the local branch of the Federation but during the campaign they repudiated him.

[4] Retired after nomination in favour of the Coalition Liberal candidate.

NATIONAL FELLOWSHIP

Formed by Edward Martell, January 1962.

Policy: Anti-socialist.

Sources: *The New Daily,* 1962—66
The Recorder, 1962—?

Elections:

1963 (20/8)	Bristol, South-East	100	E.D. Martell	4,834	19.0

See also National Party [2] and People's League for the Defence of Freedom.

NATIONAL FRONT

Formed in March 1967 by a merger of the British National Party and the League of Empire Loyalists, (q.v.).

Policy: British nationalism.

Sources: *Spearhead,* 1964 —

Elections:

1968 (28/3)	Acton	48	A. Fountaine	1,400*	5.6
1970	Battersea, South	3	T. Lamb	716*	3.2
	Deptford	10	M.C. Vaux	1,277*	5.5
	Islington, North	22	Rev. B. Green	1,232*	5.6
	Enfield, West	135	K. Taylor	1,175*	3.1
	Huddersfield, West	161	R.J. Scott	1,427*	3.5
	Ilford, South	163	M.E.L. Skeggs	727*	1.8
	Leicester, South-West	184	J.E. Kyneston	749*	2.3
	Southall	263	J.S. Shaw	1,572*	4.4
	Wolverhampton, North-East	309	Mrs. S.M. Wright	1,592*	4.7
	Cardiff, South-East	545	G.W. Parsons	982*	1.9
1970 (22/10)	St. Marylebone	35	M.E.L. Skeggs	401*	2.4
1970 (19/11)	Enfield, West	135	K. Taylor	1,176*	4.4
1972 (7/12)	Uxbridge	446	J.M. Clifton	2,920*	8.2
1973 (24/5)	West Bromwich	302	M.G.A. Webster	4,789	16.0
1973 (8/11)	Hove	159	J. Harrison-Broadley	1,409*	3.0
1974 (F)	Brent, North	11	R.A. Smith	1,570*	2.7
	Brent, South	12	J. Harrison-Broadley	1,852*	4.2
	Bromley, Ravensbourne	16	G.J. Parker	786*	2.0
	Enfield, Edmonton	30	D.J. Bruce	1,765*	3.8
	Enfield, North	31	K.T. Robinson	1,352*	2.6
	Enfield, Southgate	32	B.W. Pell	1,192*	2.2
	Greenwich, Woolwich East	34	P.S. Hanman	1,066*	2.8
	Hackney, North and Stoke Newington	37	H.C. Lord	1,226*	3.8
	Hammersmith, Fulham	39	A. Smithies	966*	2.1
	Haringey, Tottenham	42	R.W. Painter	1,270*	4.1
	Harrow, Central	44	J.A. Donin	823*	2.3
	Hillingdon, Hayes and Harlington	50	J.S. Fairhurst	2,721*	6.5
	Hounslow, Brentford and Isleworth	53	T.W. Benford	1,741*	3.1
	Hounslow, Feltham and Heston	54	Mrs. J.M. Reid	2,653*	4.4

Islington, North	56	J.W. Score	871*	3.4
Lambeth, Streatham	64	T. Lamb	937*	2.3
Lewisham, West	68	P. Williams	1,000*	2.1
Newham, South	73	M. Lobb	2,511*	6.9
Richmond upon Thames, Richmond	77	E.A. Russell	570*	1.3
Southwark, Bermondsey	79	G. Davey	1,485*	4.1
Waltham Forest, Leyton	87	Mrs. S.M. Bothwell	2,097*	4.5
Wandsworth, Battersea South	90	J.M. Clifton	787*	2.3
Birmingham, Erdington	105	T.M. Finnegan	1,145*	2.4
Birmingham, Ladywood	108	J.A.A. Davis	751*	2.9
Birmingham, Perry Barr	110	A.C. Shorthouse	853*	2.1
Blackburn	116	J.K. Read	1,778*	4.2
Bolton, East	121	G. Booth	1,259*	2.6
Bournemouth, East	124	M.J. Hayes	875*	2.0
Bristol, South	134	P.H. Gannaway	1,006*	2.2
Bristol, South-East	135	R.J. Bale	757*	1.3
Eton and Slough	161	A.P. Coniam	1,541*	3.0
Hove	177	E. Budden	442*	0.8
Huddersfield, East	178	N. Mear	796*	1.9
Leicester, East	193	W.K. Sanders	3,662*	7.4
Leicester, South	194	J.E. Knyaston	1,639*	3.0
Leicester, West	195	W.J. Newcombe	2,579*	5.3
Liverpool, Walton	203	C. Gibbon	647*	1.7
Manchester, Openshaw	213	J. Hulse	541*	1.7
Norwich, North	225	Mrs. G. Goold	544*	1.5
Rochdale	247	M.W. Sellors	1,885*	3.7
South Shields	266	W. Owen	1,958*	3.8
Spelthorne	267	E.J. Butterfield	1,399*	2.5
Watford	295	J.E. Wotherspoon	651*	1.4
West Bromwich, East	296	M.G.A. Webster	2,907*	7.0
West Bromwich, West	297	G.D. Bowen	3,107*	7.8
Wolverhampton, North-East	299	A.D.C. Webber	2,548*	5.3
Wolverhampton, South-East	300	J.C. Parker	1,546*	3.9
Wolverhampton, South-West	301	G.A. Cooper	1,523*	3.0
Aldershot	374	T. Greenslade	1,148*	1.8
Canterbury	393	K.R. McKilliam	831*	1.2
Dartford	394	R.H. Aldous	945*	2.0
Gravesend	398	J.D. Turner	1,726*	2.4
Carlton	442	C. Marriott	1,449*	2.4
Harrogate	508	A.H.W. Brons	1,186*	2.3
1974 (23/5) Newham, South	73	M. Lobb	1,713*	11.5

National Front

1974 (O)					
Barking, Barking	1	C.W. Bond	1,661*	4.9
Barnet, Chipping Barnet	3	R.A. Cole	1,207*	2.9
Barnet, Finchley	4	Mrs. J. Godfrey	993*	2.7
Brent, East	10	N.A. Lyons	1,096*	2.9
Brent, North	11	Mrs. J.O. Cattanach	1,297*	2.5
Brent, South	12	J. Harrison-Broadley	1,388*	3.7
Bromley, Ravensbourne	16	I.D. Steven	574*	1.6
City of London and Westminster South	20	Dr. D. Baxter	686*	2.5
Croydon, North-West	25	P.J. Holland	1,049*	2.7
Enfield, Edmonton	30	D.J. Bruce	1,895*	4.6
Enfield, North	31	R.D. Burton	1,330*	2.8
Enfield, Southgate	32	B.W. Pell	1,255*	2.6
Greenwich, Woolwich East	34	M.E.L. Skeggs	1,000*	3.1
Hackney, North and Stoke Newington	37	H.C. Lord	1,044*	3.7
Hackney, South and Shoreditch	38	R. May	2,544*	9.4
Hammersmith, Fulham	39	J. Cordrey	855*	2.1
Haringey, Hornsey	41	Mrs. J. Stubbs	973*	2.4
Haringey, Tottenham	42	R.W. Painter	2,211*	8.3
Haringey, Wood Green	43	K. Squire	2,603*	8.0
Harrow, Central	44	C.A. Byrne	813*	2.5
Hillingdon, Hayes and Harlington	50	J.S. Fairhurst	1,189*	3.1
Hounslow, Brentford and Isleworth	53	T.W. Benford	1,362*	2.6
Hounslow, Feltham and Heston	54	Mrs. J.M. Reid	1,984*	3.7
Islington, Central	55	J.W. Score	1,335*	5.3
Lambeth, Streatham	64	T. Lamb	817*	2.3
Lewisham, Deptford	66	R.C. Edmonds	1,731*	4.8
Lewisham, West	68	P. Williams	1,114*	2.5
Newham, North-East	71	J.B. Newham	2,715*	6.9
Newham, South	73	E.O. Bayly	2,412*	7.8
Richmond upon Thames, Richmond	77	E.A. Russell	1,000*	2.5
Southwark, Bermondsey	79	G. Davey	1,488*	4.8
Tower Hamlets, Bethnal Green and Bow	84	W.E. Castleton	2,172*	7.6
Waltham Forest, Leyton	87	Mrs. S.M. Bothwell	2,168*	5.4
Waltham Forest, Walthamstow	88	R. Adde	1,911*	5.5

Wandsworth, Battersea North	89	R.F. Friend	1,250*	4.5
Accrington	93	D.A. Riley	1,176*	2.9
Birmingham, Erdington	105	T.M. Finnegan	1,413*	3.3
Birmingham, Handsworth	107	J. Finnegan	838*	2.8
Birmingham, Perry Barr	110	R.J. Warren	826*	2.1
Birmingham, Yardley	115	H. Challender	1,034*	2.4
Blackburn	116	J.K. Read	1,758*	4.4
Bolton, East	121	G. Booth	1,106*	2.4
Bolton, West	122	W.H. Roberts	1,072*	2.7
Bournemouth, East	124	M.J. Hayes	828*	2.1
Bristol, South	134	P.H. Gannaway	795*	1.9
Bristol, South-East	135	R.J. Bale	775*	1.5
Coventry, South-West	149	R. Rickard	822*	1.5
Dudley, East	156	C.R. Knott	1,171*	2.9
Eton and Slough	161	A.P. Coniam	1,241*	2.7
Fareham	163	R.M. Doughty	617*	1.4
Gillingham	167	S.G. Campbell	922*	2.0
Huddersfield, East	178	J.D. Robertshaw	764*	2.0
Huddersfield, West	179	D. Ford	760*	1.9
Keighley	183	G.K. Wright	859*	2.0
Leicester, East	193	P.A.F. Reed-Herbert	2,967*	6.4
Leicester, South	194	A.R. Cartwright	2,072*	4.1
Leicester, West	195	W.J. Newcombe	2,253*	5.1
Manchester, Blackley	209	H. Andrew	914*	2.4
Nottingham, North	228	D. Caine	792*	1.5
Oxford	233	I.H.M. Anderson	572*	1.1
Preston, South	243	E.V. Harrison	663*	1.7
Reading, North	245	P. Baker	594*	1.3
Rochdale	247	M.W. Sellors	1,927*	4.1
Rochester and Chatham	248	G.T. Hazelden	1,150*	1.9
Sheffield, Heeley	257	P.J. Revell	723*	1.5
South Shields	266	W. Owen	711*	1.5
Spelthorne	267	J.M. Clifton	1,180*	2.3
Thanet, East	282	K. Munson	708*	2.1
Wallasey	288	J. Fishwick	787*	1.5
Walsall, South	291	J.C. Parker	1,226*	2.8
Watford	295	J.E. Wotherspoon	671*	1.5
West Bromwich, East	296	G.D. Bowen	1,692*	4.3
West Bromwich, West	297	R. Churms	2,022*	5.4
Wolverhampton, North-East	299	A.D.C. Webber	1,928*	4.2
Wolverhampton, South-East	300	G.F. Oldland	1,703*	4.7

National Front

1974 (O) (cont.)					
	Wolverhampton, South-West	301	G.A. Cooper	1,573*	3.3
	Wycombe	317	D. Howard-Smith	2,049*	3.5
	Aldershot	374	T. Greenslade	1,120*	1.9
	Basingstoke	375	E.A. Goodall	763*	1.1
	Hertford and Stevenage	384	K. Taylor	1,232*	2.0
	Canterbury	393	K.R. McKilliam	1,096*	1.8
	Dartford	394	R.H. Aldous	939*	2.1
	Gravesend	398	J.D. Turner	1,304*	1.9
	Loughborough	419	W.K. Sanders	1,215*	2.2
	Carlton	442	C. Marriott	1,273*	2.3
	Woking	474	R.J. Vaughan-Smith	921*	1.9
	Horsham and Crawley	482	A.P. Brewer	1,101*	1.5
	Bridlington	496	F.H. Day	987*	2.2
	Harrogate	508	A.H.W. Brons	1,030*	2.3
	Glasgow, Govan	569	M.A.B. Brooks	86*	0.4

NATIONAL INDEPENDENCE PARTY

Formed in July 1972 by, among others, former members of the National Front.

Policy: British nationalism.

Sources: *The Independent*, 1972—

Elections:

1972 (7/12)	Sutton and Cheam	281	E. Scruby	660*	1.9
1972 (7/12)	Uxbridge	446	Miss C. Macdonald	551*	1.5
1974 (F)	Haringey, Tottenham	42	M.P. Coney	1,373*	4.4

NATIONAL LABOUR PARTY

Formed by John Bean in May 1958. In February 1960 the party merged with Colin Jordan's White Defence League to form a new party, the British National Party (q.v.) which in 1967 merged into the National Front (q.v.)

Policy: British nationalism.

Sources: Cross, Colin, *The Fascists in Britain.* 1961
Thayer, George, *The British Political Fringe.* 1965
Combat 1958–60

Elections:

1959	St. Pancras, North	36	W. Webster	1,685*	4.1

NATIONAL PARTY [1]

Formed, by Henry Page Croft, M.P. in August and September 1917. In April 1921 the
party ceased political activities and was re-named the National Constitutional Association.

Policy: Right-wing Conservatism.

Sources: Croft, Lord, *My Life of Strife.* 1948
National Opinion, 1918—23
Morning Post, 1917—21
The Times, 1917—21

Secessions: [1] The following Conservative MPs joined the party when it was formed:
A.H. Burgoyne (Kensington, North); Hon. D.G. Carnegie (Winchester);
Sir R.A. Cooper (Walsall); H.P. Croft (Christchurch); Viscount Duncannon
(Dover); Hon. E.A. Fitzroy (Northamptonshire, Southern); R. Hunt
(Ludlow); R.H. Rawson (Reigate).

Elections:

1917 (23/10)	Islington, East	21	E.B. Barnard	513	10.8
1918	Bethnal Green, North-East	5	W.L. Steel	2,312	29.3
	Hammersmith, North	21	J.C. Walker	2,075	16.7
	Hampstead	23	J.H. Wrentmore	1,881*	9.9
	Islington, East	25	C.E. Copplestone	575*	3.0
	Kensington, South	30	E. Makins	5,306	33.2
	Paddington, North	37	W.S.G. Aston	4,029	23.4
	Shoreditch	45	T. Warwick	504*	3.0
	Stepney, Limehouse	49	C.H. Rodwell	1,455	14.9
	Wandsworth, Putney	56	Hon. J.G. Jenkins	4,968	36.4
	Wandsworth, Streatham	57	F.H. Bellamy	1,844*	11.7
	Bournemouth	92	†H.P. Croft [2]	14,048	66.3
	Bristol, North	100	E.W. Petter	2,520	13.3
	East Ham, North	123	W. Mann	6,748	41.7
	Leeds, North	153	H.F. Wyatt	1,282*	6.9
	Manchester, Ardwick	176	H.M. Stephenson	3,510	19.7
	Nottingham, Central	198	A. Kitson	1,999*	12.1
	Rochdale	213	J.F. Jones	1,992*	6.6
	Tynemouth	246	D. Scott	517*	3.1
	Walsall	250	†Sir R.A. Cooper, Bt. [2]	14,491	52.3
	Thornbury	345	T.D. Pilcher	6,132	38.0
	Hertford	356	E.B. Barnard [3]	7,158	38.8
	Chislehurst	365	A. Edmunds	2,507	23.2
	Gravesend	369	H. Hinckley	985*	6.5
	Kettering	420	A.F.H. Ferguson	4,489	19.9

National Party [1]

1918	Frome	438	T.M.H. Kincaid-Smith	258*	1.1
(cont.)	Wells	440	G.C.S. Hodgson	804*	4.6
1919 (7/10)	Manchester, Rusholme	184	R.B. Crewdson	815*	4.0
1920 (27/3)	Dartford	366	R.V.K. Applin[4]	2,952*	10.9

[1] Of the eight MPs who adhered to the National Party when it was formed, Burgoyne and Fitzroy resigned within a few months. Rawson died and the seat was vacant at the Dissolution in 1918. The relationship of Hunt and Duncannon with the party during the latter part of 1918 is unclear but both appear to have been in good standing with their local Conservative Associations at the time of the Dissolution. Hunt did not seek re-election due to ill-health but Duncannon was returned as a Conservative supporter of the Coalition. Carnegie intended to stand as a National Party candidate but withdrew after the local Conservative Association decided to adopt a candidate to oppose him. Cooper and Croft were both re-elected but without Conservative opposition.

[2] Re-joined the Conservative Party in April 1921.

[3] Also the nominee of the National Farmers' Union.

[4] Also supported by Horatio Bottomley's Independent Parliamentary Group.

NATIONAL PARTY [2]

Formed by Edward Martell, September 1966.

Policy: Anti-socialist.

Sources: *The New Daily,* 1966

Elections:

1967 (9/3)   Nuneaton   507   D.C.T. Bennett   517*   1.2

See also National Fellowship and People's League for the Defence of Freedom.

NATIONAL PROHIBITION PARTY

Formed, at a convention held in London, December 1887. Affiliated to the World Prohibition Federation. The party continued activities until about 1949 after which it appears to have disbanded.

Policy: Prohibition of intoxicating drink.

Sources: *National Prohibition Party Bulletin*, 1925–33
    Prohibitionist, 1933–49

Elections:

1923 (8/2)   Stepney, Whitechapel and
       St. George's   51   S.M. Holden   130*   0.9

NATIONAL SOCIALIST PARTY

Formed, in June 1916, as the result of a split in the British Socialist Party (q.v.) when pro-war members led by H.M. Hyndman resigned from the BSP to form a new party. The NSP affiliated to the Labour Party in August 1918 and reverted to its old name of Social Democratic Federation (q.v.) in August 1920.

Policy: Socialism.

Sources: Lee, H.W. & Archbold, E., *Social Democracy in Great Britain.* 1935
Tsuzuki, C., *H.M. Hyndman and British Socialism.* 1961
*Justice, 1916—20

Elections:

1918	Burnley	104	†D.D. Irving[1]	15,217	41.9
	Reading	211	L.E. Quelch	1,462*	5.2
	West Ham, Silvertown	259	†J.J. Jones[2]	6,971	51.6
	Romford	338	A. Whiting	2,580	14.4

For elections results from 1920 see Social Democratic Federation.

[1] Secured Labour Party endorsement.
[2] Joined the Labour Party, February 1919.

NATIONAL UNION OF SMALL SHOPKEEPERS

Formed as a trade union in 1943.

Policy: To safeguard the interests of small shopkeepers.

Sources: *Small Shopkeeper*, 1943–

Elections:

1959 (19/3)	Harrow, East	149	T. Lynch	348*	1.0
1962 (17/4)	Derby, North	122	T. Lynch	886*	2.7
1968 (31/10)	Bassetlaw	461	T. Lynch	1,053*	2.4

NEW CONSERVATIVE PARTY

Formed by John E. Dayton in March 1960. Re-named True Conservative Party, May 1961.
The party was dissolved in the autumn of 1961 when Dayton formed a new organisation
which he called the Patriotic Front for Political Action. In February 1962 he joined the
Labour Party.

Policy: British nationalism.

Sources: *Watching Brief,* 1960—61

Elections:

1960 (17/3)	Harrow, West	150	J.E. Dayton	1,560*	4.7
1960 (16/11)	Bolton, East	82	J.E. Dayton	493*	1.2
1960 (16/11)	Bedfordshire, Mid	317	C.F.H. Gilliard	235*	0.6
1961 (8/11)	Oswestry	470	J.E. Dayton[1]	839*	2.8

[1] As a candidate of the Patriotic Front.

NEW PARTY

Formed by Sir Oswald Mosley in February 1931. Merged in the British Union of Fascists when that organisation was formed in October 1932.

Policy: At first advocating a 'National Policy' to meet the economic crisis, the party later moved towards fascism.

Sources: Benewick, Robert, *The Fascist Movement in Britain.* 1972
Cross, Colin, *The Fascists in Britain.* 1961
Nicolson, Nigel, *Harold Nicolson Diaries and Letters 1930–39.* 1966
*Action, October/December 1931

Secessions: The following Labour MPs joined the New Party when it was formed:
Dr. R. Forgan (Renfrewshire, Western). Lady Cynthia Mosley (Stoke-on-Trent, Stoke); Sir O.E. Mosley, Bt. (Smethwick); E.J. St.L. Strachey (Birmingham, Aston). In addition, O. Baldwin (Dudley) and W.J. Brown (Wolverhampton, West) who had been associated with Mosley, resigned from the Labour Party but almost immediately disassociated themselves from the New Party and were never actual members of the parliamentary group.
One Ulster Unionist MP, W.E.D. Allen (Belfast, West) also seceded and immediately following the announcement of the 1931 Dissolution, a Liberal MP, C.R. Dudgeon (Galloway) joined the party.
Strachey resigned from the New Party in July 1931 and Allen did not seek re-election at the General Election of 1931.

Elections:

1931 (30/4)	Ashton-under-Lyne	64	A. Young	4,472	16.0
1931	Battersea, South	2	L.J. Cuming	909*	2.2
	Hammersmith, North	21	R.E.N. Braden	431*	1.4
	Stepney, Limehouse	49	H.L. Hodge	307*	1.4
	Stepney, Whitechapel and St. George's	51	E. Lewis	154*	0.7
	Wandsworth, Central	54	A.M. Diston	424*	1.6
	Ashton-under-Lyne	64	C.B. Hobhouse	424*	1.4
	Birmingham, Duddeston	76	J. Williams	284*	1.1
	Birmingham, Yardley	85	E.J. Bartleet	479*	1.0
	Gateshead	128	J.S. Barr	1,077*	1.9
	Manchester, Hulme	181	Sir J.W. Pratt	1,565*	4.4
	Reading	211	E.R. Troward	861*	1.6
	Rochester, Chatham	214	M.F. Woodroffe	1,135*	3.6
	Sheffield, Brightside	224	E.C. Snelgrove	847*	2.2.
	Stoke-on-Trent, Stoke	240	Sir O.E. Mosley, Bt.	10,534	24.1

Derbyshire, North-Eastern	307	A.V. Williams	689* 1.7
Shipley	508	W.J. Leaper	601* 1.4
Merthyr Tydfil, Merthyr	518	S. Davies	10,834 30.6
Pontypridd	539	W. Lowell	466* 1.3
Glasgow, Cathcart	561	J. Mellick	529* 1.5
Glasgow, Shettleston	571	W.E. Stevenson	402* 1.2
Galloway	595	C.R. Dudgeon	986* 3.0
Coatbridge	600	W.W. Gilmour	674* 2.1
Renfrewshire, Western	614	Dr. R. Forgan	1,304* 4.0
Combined English Universities	628	Hon. H.G. Nicolson	461* 3.4

PATRIOTIC PARTY

Formed, as The True Tories, by Major-General Richard Hilton in 1962. In 1964 the organisation changed its name to the Patriotic Party. During the General Election campaign of 1964 the party split and Major-General Hilton's supporters reverted to the original name The True Tories while the Deputy Chairman, Major Arthur Braybrooke, continued the Patriotic Party as his organisation. Both The True Tories and the Patriotic Party subsequently merged with the National Front (q.v.) after it was formed in 1967.

Policy: British nationalism.

Sources: *A Short History of Right Wing Disunity. Liverpool Newsletter,* January 1973.

Elections:

1964	Fulham	11	A.R. Braybrooke	632*	1.8
	Dorking	491	Mrs. B. Davies	476*	1.1
1966	Fulham	11	A.R. Braybrooke	126*	0.4

PEOPLE

Formed in Coventry, January 1973.

Policy: Conservation of the environment.

Sources: *A Future for our Children; An Environment Fit for People.* (Leaflet), 1974
Ecologist, 1969–

Elections:

1974 (F)[1]	Havering, Hornchurch	47	B. Percy-Davis	619*	1.3
	Coventry, North-East	146	A.H. Pickard	1,332*	2.8
	Coventry, North-West	147	Mrs. A.L. Whittaker	1,542*	3.9
	Leeds, North-East	188	C.R. Lord	300*	0.7
	Liverpool, West Derby	205	D.B. Pascoe	388*	0.9
	Eye	466	E. Goldsmith	395*	0.7
1974 (O)	Havering, Hornchurch	47	B. Percy-Davis	797*	1.8
	Havering, Romford	48	L.H.C. Sampson	200*	0.5
	Birmingham, Northfield	109	Mrs. E.A. Davenport	359*	0.7
	Coventry, North-West	147	Mrs. A.L. Whittaker	313*	0.8
	Leeds, East	187	Mrs. N. Russell	327*	0.7

[1] In addition to the six official candidates, M. Newman, a member of People contested Birmingham, Northfield as an Independent candidate and polled 1,237* votes (2.2%).

PEOPLE'S LEAGUE FOR THE DEFENCE OF FREEDOM

Formed by Edward Martell, March 1956.

Policy: Anti-socialist.

Sources: *The People's Guardian*, 1956– ?
          The New Daily, 1965–66

Elections:

1957 (30/5)	East Ham, North	130	E.D. Martell	2,730*	12.2

See also National Fellowship and National Party [2].

PLAID CYMRU

Formed by John Saunders Lewis (of the University College, Swansea), August 1925. The
title of the party (pronounced Plide Cumree) translates from Welsh as 'Party of Wales' or
the 'Welsh Party'.

Policy: Welsh nationalism.

Sources: Coupland, Sir Reginald, *Welsh and Scottish Nationalism.* 1954
Jones, J.E., *Tros Gymru.* 1970
Various authors, *The Historical Basis of Welsh Nationalism.* 1950
Welsh Nationalist, 1932–49
Welsh Nation, 1949–

Elections:

1929	Caernarvonshire	526	Rev. L.E. Valentine	609*	1.6
1931	Caernarvonshire	526	Prof. J.E. Daniel	1,136*	3.0
	University of Wales	631	J.S. Lewis	914	29.1
1935	Caernarvonshire	526	Prof. J.E. Daniel	2,534*	6.9
1943 (29/1)	University of Wales	631	J.S. Lewis	1,330	22.5
1945 (26/4)	Caernarvon Boroughs	513	Prof. J.E. Daniel	6,844	24.8
1945 (15/5)	Neath	537	W.I. Samuel	6,290	16.2
1945	Caernarvon Boroughs	513	Prof. J.E. Daniel	1,560*	4.5
	Rhondda, East	520	J.K. Davies	2,123*	6.1
	Caernarvonshire	526	W.A. Bebb	2,152*	5.4
	Neath	537	W.I. Samuel	3,659*	7.3
	Ogmore	538	T.R. Morgan	2,379*	5.6
	Merionethshire	540	G.R. Evans	2,448*	10.3
	University of Wales	631	Dr. Gwenan Jones	1,696	24.5
1946 (4/6)	Ogmore	538	T.R. Morgan	5,685	29.4
1946 (5/12)	Merthyr Tydfil, Aberdare	517	W.I. Samuel	7,090	20.0
1950	Aberdare	543	W.I. Samuel	3,310*	7.4
	Rhondda, East	549	D. Davies	1,357*	3.9
	Rhondda, West	550	J.K. Davies	2,183*	6.6
	Caernarvon	555	J.E. Jones	4,882	13.1
	Llanelli	559	Rev. D.E. Morgan	2,134*	3.8
	Wrexham	561	G. Bowen	960*	1.7
	Merionethshire	571	G.R. Evans	2,754*	11.1
1951	Aberdare	543	W.I. Samuel	2,691*	6.1
	Rhondda, West	550	J.K. Davies	2,467*	7.7
	Llanelli	559	Rev. D.E. Morgan	3,765*	6.9
	Wrexham	561	A.D. Thomas	1,997*	3.6
1954 (28/10)	Aberdare	543	G.R. Evans	5,671	16.0
1955 (17/3)	Wrexham	561	D.E. Morgan	4,572*	11.3

Plaid Cymru

1955	Aberdare	543	T. Beasley	3,703*	9.4
	Rhondda, West	550	G.P. James	4,424	15.3
	Anglesey	553	J.R. Jones	2,183*	7.5
	Caernarvon	555	R.E. Jones	5,815	16.5
	Conway	556	I.B. Rees	3,019*	7.8
	Carmarthen	558	Mrs. J.E. Davies	3,835*	7.8
	Llanelli	559	Rev. D.E. Morgan	6,398	12.5
	Wrexham	561	D.E. Morgan	5,139*	10.4
	Gower	567	E.C. Rees	4,101*	10.6
	Merionethshire	571	G.R. Evans	5,243	22.1
	Abertillery	572	T.R. Morgan	1,259*	4.1
1956 (6/7)	Newport	548	E.P. Roberts	1,978*	3.8
1957 (28/2)	Carmarthen	558	Mrs. J.E. Davies	5,741*	11.5
1958 (10/11)	Pontypool	576	B.C.L. Morgan	2,927*	10.0
1959	Aberdare	543	K.P. Thomas	3,367*	8.2
	Cardiff, North	544	E.P. Roberts	2,553*	5.1
	Rhondda, East	549	N.O. Williams	2,776*	8.8
	Rhondda, West	550	G.P. James	4,978	17.0
	Swansea, East	551	E.C. Rees	4,651*	10.5
	Anglesey	553	Dr. R.T. Jones	4,121	14.6
	Caernarvon	555	D.O. Jones	7,293	21.2
	Conway	556	I.B. Rees	2,852*	7.6
	Cardiganshire	557	G.W. Evans	3,880	12.8
	Carmarthen	558	H.H. Roberts	2,545*	5.2
	Llanelli	559	Rev. D.E. Morgan	7,176	13.8
	Denbigh	560	Dr. D.A. Jones	3,077*	7.2
	Wrexham	561	D.E. Morgan	6,579*	12.2
	Flintshire, West	563	E.N.C. Williams	1,594*	4.1
	Aberavon	564	I.M. Lewis	3,066*	6.6
	Caerphilly	566	J.D.A. Howell	3,420*	8.8
	Gower	567	Dr. J.G. Griffiths	3,744*	9.1
	Merionethshire	571	G.R. Evans	5,127	22.9
	Pontypool	576	B.C.L. Morgan	2,519*	6.6
	Pembrokeshire	578	W.G. Williams	2,253*	4.3
1960 (17/11)	Ebbw Vale	574	E.P. Roberts	2,091*	7.0
1962 (15/5)	Montgomeryshire	577	Rev. I.F. Elis	1,594*	6.2
1963 (28/3)	Swansea, East	551	E.C. Rees	1,620*	5.2
1964	Aberdare	543	D.W.H. Thomas	2,723*	7.2
	Cardiff, North	544	E.P. Roberts	1,058*	2.2
	Merthyr Tydfil	547	I.B. Rees	2,878*	9.3
	Rhondda, East	549	G.P. James	2,361*	8.2
	Rhondda, West	550	H.V. Davies	2,668*	10.2

	Swansea, East	551	E.C. Rees	3,556*	8.4
	Anglesey	553	Dr. R.T. Jones	1,817*	6.5
	Breconshire and Radnorshire	554	T.R. Morgan	2,165*	5.2
	Caernarvon	555	R.E. Jones	6,998	21.4
	Conway	556	G. Hughes	3,058*	8.3
	Cardiganshire	557	G.W. Evans	3,262*	10.9
	Carmarthen	558	G.R. Evans	5,495*	11.7
	Llanelli	559	Dr. W.T.P. Davies	3,469*	7.0
	Denbigh	560	Dr. D.A. Jones	3,444*	7.9
	Wrexham	561	J.R. Thomas	4,673*	8.9
	Flintshire, West	563	E.N.C. Williams	1,195*	3.0
	Aberavon	564	G. John	2,118*	4.6
	Caerphilly	566	P.J.S. Williams	3,956*	11.0
	Gower	567	Dr. J.G. Griffiths	2,562*	6.5
	Ogmore	569	Mrs. M. Tucker	2,470*	5.3
	Merionethshire	571	D.E. Morgan	3,697	16.8
	Montgomeryshire	577	Rev. I.F. Elis	2,167*	8.5
	Pembrokeshire	578	D. Thomas	1,717*	3.4
1965 (1/4)	Abertillery	572	E.J. Merriman	1,551*	6.7
1966	Aberdare	543	J.E.W. Williams	3,073*	8.6
	Merthyr Tydfil	547	M. Stephens	3,361*	11.5
	Rhondda, East	549	G.P. James	2,088*	7.5
	Rhondda, West	550	H.V. Davies	2,172*	8.7
	Swansea, East	551	E.C. Rees	2,749*	6.8
	Anglesey	553	J.W. Meredith	2,596*	9.6
	Breconshire and Radnorshire	554	T.R. Morgan	2,410*	6.0
	Caernarvon	555	H. Roberts	6,834	21.7
	Conway	556	R.E. Jones	2,552*	6.6
	Cardiganshire	557	E.G. Millward	2,469*	8.1
	Carmarthen	558	G.R. Evans	7,416	16.1
	Llanelli	559	Dr. W.T.P. Davies	5,132*	10.9
	Denbigh	560	W.M. Edwards	2,695*	6.1
	Wrexham	561	J.R. Thomas	2,297*	4.5
	Flintshire, East	562	G. Hughes	902*	1.9
	Flintshire, West	563	D.A. Lloyd	1,585*	3.8
	Caerphilly	566	J.D.A. Howell	3,949*	11.1
	Merionethshire	571	I.L. Jenkins	2,490*	11.4
	Montgomeryshire	577	T. Edwards	1,841*	7.4
	Pembrokeshire	578	J. Sheppard	2,460*	5.0
1966 (14/7)	Carmarthen	558	†G.R. Evans	16,179	39.0
1967 (9/3)	Rhondda, West	550	H.V. Davies	10,067	39.9

Plaid Cymru

1968 (18/7)	Caerphilly	566	Dr. P.J.S. Williams	14,274	40.4
1970	Aberdare	543	Dr. G.M. Jones	11,431	30.0
	Cardiff, North	544	B.M. Edwards	1,927*	4.1
	Cardiff, South-East	545	R.B. Davies	2,585*	5.1
	Cardiff, West	546	Dr. D. Hughes	4,378*	10.1
	Merthyr Tydfil	547	E.C. Rees	3,076*	9.6
	Newport	548	A.R. Vickery	1,997*	3.7
	Rhondda, East	549	G.P. James	6,931	24.3
	Rhondda, West	550	H.V. Davies	3,528	14.0
	Swansea, East	551	D.R. Evans	4,188*	10.2
	Swansea, West	552	G.R. ap Gwent	3,033*	6.2
	Anglesey	553	J.L. Williams	7,140	22.1
	Breconshire and Radnorshire	554	W.G. Jenkins	2,349*	5.4
	Caernarvon	555	J.R.J. Lewis	11,331	33.4
	Conway	556	D.E. Thomas	4,311*	10.8
	Cardiganshire	557	H.W.J. ap Robert	6,498	19.6
	Carmarthen	558	G.R. Evans	14,812	30.1
	Llanelli	559	C.R. James	8,387	16.8
	Denbigh	560	E.G. Matthews	5,254*	11.0
	Wrexham	561	C. Golding	2,894*	5.3
	Flintshire, East	562	G. Hughes	2,332*	4.4
	Flintshire, West	563	Dr. A.O. Jones	3,108*	6.9
	Aberavon	564	G. Farmer	3,912*	8.4
	Barry	565	E.O. Williams	4,200*	7.1
	Caerphilly	566	Dr. P.J.S. Williams	11,505	28.5
	Gower	567	C.G. Davies	5,869	14.0
	Neath	568	G. John	4,012*	10.1
	Ogmore	569	E.J. Merriman	5,828*	11.7
	Pontypridd	570	D.E. Jones	5,059*	10.4
	Merionethshire	571	D.W. Wigley	5,425	24.3
	Abertillery	572	D.B. Harries	1,751*	6.2
	Bedwellty	573	C.M. Davey	3,780*	10.0
	Ebbw Vale	574	D.J. Baskerville	1,805*	6.0
	Monmouth	575	S.K. Neale	1,501*	2.5
	Pontypool	576	H. Webb	2,053*	5.3
	Montgomeryshire	577	E.G. Millward	3,145*	11.8
	Pembrokeshire	578	W.I. Samuel	3,681*	6.7
1972 (13/4)	Merthyr Tydfil	547	E.P. Roberts	11,852	37.0
1974 (F)	Aberdare	517	G.E. Owen	11,973	30.0
	Cardiff, North	518	P.B. Richards	1,586*	4.6
	Cardiff, North-West	519	C.F. Palfrey	1,227*	3.4

Cardiff, South-East	520	K. Bush	1,254*	3.0
Cardiff, West	521	Dr. D. Hughes	2,093*	5.5
Merthyr Tydfil	522	E.P. Roberts	7,336	22.9
Newport	523	Mrs. P.M. Cox	936*	1.6
Rhondda	524	G.P. James	6,739	12.9
Swansea, East	525	J.G. Ball	5,135*	11.9
Swansea, West	526	D.K. Hearne	1,859*	3.6
Anglesey	527	D. Iwan	7,610	21.7
Breconshire and Radnorshire	528	D.N. Gittins	2,099*	4.7
Caernarvon	529	†D.W. Wigley	14,103	40.5
Conway	530	P.M. Farmer	4,203*	10.1
Cardiganshire	531	C.G. Davies	4,754	13.3
Carmarthen	532	G.R. Evans	17,162	34.3
Llanelli	533	W.R. Williams	6,020*	12.0
Denbigh	534	E.G. Matthews	4,103*	8.1
Wrexham	535	H.W. Roberts	2,624*	4.5
Flintshire, East	536	N.H. Taylor	1,135*	1.9
Flintshire, West	537	G. Hughes	2,296*	4.4
Aberavon	538	Rev. G.G. Foster	5,898*	12.2
Barry	539	Mrs. V. Wynne-Williams	1,924*	3.4
Caerphilly	540	Dr. P.J.S. Williams	11,956	27.6
Gower	541	J.N. Harris	3,741*	8.3
Neath	542	H.G. Evans	8,758	21.5
Ogmore	543	E.J. Merriman	5,139*	9.6
Pontypridd	544	R.A. Kemp	4,612*	8.6
Merionethshire	545	†D.E. Thomas	7,823	34.6
Abertillery	546	W.A. Richards	3,119*	10.9
Bedwellty	547	A. Moore	3,048*	7.7
Ebbw Vale	548	J.D. Rogers	1,767*	5.9
Monmouth	549	E.H. Spanswick	930*	1.5
Pontypool	550	R.D. Tanner	1,318*	3.1
Montgomeryshire	551	A. Jones	2,274*	8.3
Pembrokeshire	552	R.B. Davies	2,820*	4.8
1974 (O) Aberdare	517	G.E. Owen	8,133	21.3
Cardiff, North	518	P.B. Richards	1,464*	4.6
Cardiff, North-West	519	C.F. Palfrey	1,278*	3.7
Cardiff, South-East	520	K. Bush	983*	2.4
Cardiff, West	521	Dr. D. Hughes	2,008*	5.5
Merthyr Tydfil	522	E.P. Roberts	4,455	14.8
Newport	523	G. Lee	1,216*	2.1

Plaid Cymru

1974 (O) (cont.)					
	Rhondda	524	D. Morgan	4,173*	8.3
	Swansea, East	525	J.G. Ball	3,978*	9.5
	Swansea, West	526	G.R. ap Gwent	1,778*	3.6
	Anglesey	527	D. Iwan	6,410	19.1
	Breconshire and Radnorshire	528	D.N. Gittins	2,300*	5.2
	Caernarvon	529	†D.W. Wigley	14,624	42.6
	Conway	530	P.M. Farmer	4,668*	11.8
	Cardiganshire	531	C.G. Davies	4,583	13.2
	Carmarthen	532	†G.R. Evans	23,325	45.1
	Llanelli	533	W.R. Williams	6,797	13.7
	Denbigh	534	I.W. Jones	5,754*	11.9
	Wrexham	535	H.W. Roberts	2,859*	5.1
	Flintshire, East	536	F. Evans	1,779*	3.2
	Flintshire, West	537	N.H. Taylor	2,306*	4.8
	Aberavon	538	D.G. Thomas	4,032*	8.5
	Barry	539	Mrs. V. Wynne-Williams	1,793*	3.3
	Caerphilly	540	Dr. P.J.S. Williams	10,452	24.5
	Gower	541	M. Powell	4,369*	10.0
	Neath	542	H.G. Evans	7,305	17.9
	Ogmore	543	D.I. Jones	4,290*	8.4
	Pontypridd	544	R.A. Kemp	3,917*	7.6
	Merionethshire	545	†D.E. Thomas	9,543	42.5
	Abertillery	546	A. Richards	2,480*	9.0
	Bedwellty	547	Dr. D.J. Mogford	3,086*	8.0
	Ebbw Vale	548	Dr. G. ap Robert	2,101*	7.3
	Monmouth	549	T.F. Brimmacombe	839*	1.4
	Pontypool	550	R.D. Tanner	2,223*	5.6
	Montgomeryshire	551	A. Jones	2,440*	9.3
	Pembrokeshire	552	R.B. Davies	2,580*	4.5

RADICAL ALLIANCE

Formed in August 1965 by a group of supporters of the Campaign for Nuclear Disarmament. The organisation appears to have disbanded after the General Election of 1966.

Policy: Pacifism.

Sources: Hart-Davis, Duff, *Thorn in the Left Flank. Sunday Telegraph,*
                January 23, 1966

Elections:

1966 (27/1)	Kingston upon Hull, North	170	R.W. Gott	253*	0.5
1966	Fulham	11	Miss M.P. Arrowsmith	163*	0.5

REVOLUTIONARY COMMUNIST PARTY

Formed (as the British Section of the Fourth International) at a conference in London, March 1944 when members of the Workers' International League and the Revolutionary League merged to form a new party. The party was dissolved in July 1949 and an official statement said that members would now join the Labour Party.

Policy: Communism (Trotskyist).

Sources: *Socialist Appeal,* 1944—49

Elections:

1945 (15/5)   Neath   537   J.R. Haston   1,781*   4.6

SCOTTISH LABOUR PARTY

Formed, in January 1900 (as the Scottish Workers' Parliamentary Elections Committee),
at a conference in Edinburgh of representatives of trade unions, trades councils, co-operative
societies and socialist societies. Re-named the Scottish Workers' Representation Committee
shortly after it was formed. Following the General Election of 1906, the Committee
affiliated to the Labour Party and changed its name to the Scottish Labour Party. At
its annual conference in January 1909 it was decided to merge with the Labour Party.

Policy: Socialism.

Sources: Bealey, Frank & Pelling, Henry, *Labour and Politics 1900–1906*. 1958
                 Marwick, W.H., *A Short History of Labour in Scotland*. 1967

Elections:

1900	Glasgow, Camlachie	482	A.E. Fletcher	3,107	41.7
1901 (26/9)	Lanarkshire, North-Eastern	522	R. Smillie	2,900	21.7
1904 (10/8)	Lanarkshire, North-Eastern	522	J. Robertson	3,984	27.9
1906	Falkirk Burghs	479	D. Gilmour	1,763	17.5
	Paisley	494	R. Smillie	2,482	23.1
	Ayrshire, Northern	502	J. Brown	2,683	20.8
	Lanarkshire, North-Eastern	522	J. Robertson	4,658	29.2
	Lanarkshire, North-Western	523	J. Sullivan	3,291	23.9
1908 (9/5)	Dundee	473	G.H. Stuart	4,014	24.9
1908 (12/5)	Montrose Burghs	493	J. Burgess	1,937	29.4

D

SCOTTISH LAND RESTORATION LEAGUE

Formed in Glasgow, February 1884. The formation of the League was influenced by the visit to Scotland in 1884 of Henry George the American land reformer. The history of the League is obscure but it is likely that it subsequently became the Scottish Single Tax League which in 1904 changed its name to the Scottish League for the Taxation of Land Values.

Policy: The restoration of the land to the people.

Sources: Marwick, W.H., *A Short History of Labour in Scotland.* 1967

Elections:

1885					
	Glasgow, Blackfriars and Hutchesontown	480	J.S. Maxwell	1,156	14.4
	Glasgow, Bridgeton	481	W. Forsyth	978	12.1
	Glasgow, Tradeston	486	W.M. Greaves	86	1.1
	Greenock	487	J.M. Davidson	65	1.1
	Partick	524	J. Murdoch	74	1.0

SCOTTISH NATIONAL PARTY

Formed, as the National Party of Scotland, April 1928. The party came into being as the result of a series of conferences attended by delegates from various home-rule and nationalist bodies who agreed to merge and form a new party. The party was re-named Scottish National Party on being joined by the Scottish Party (q.v.) in April 1934.

Policy: Scottish nationalism.

Sources: Coupland, Sir Reginald, *Welsh and Scottish Nationalism.* 1954
Hanham, H.J., *Scottish Nationalism.* 1969
Kellas, James G., *Modern Scotland; The Nation since 1870.* 1968
Kellas, James G., *The Scottish Political System.* 1973
MacCormick, J.M., *The Flag in the Wind.* 1955
McLean, Iain, *Scottish Nationalism.* B. Phil. Thesis, Oxford, 1969
Scots Independent, 1926–

Elections:

1929 (29/1)	Midlothian and Peeblesshire, Northern	607	J.L.T.C. Spence	842*	4.5
1929	Glasgow, Camlachie	560	J.M. MacCormick	1,646*	4.9
	Renfrewshire, Western	614	R.E. Muirhead	1,667*	5.4
1930 (26/6)	Glasgow, Shettleton	571	J.M. McNicol	2,527*	10.1
1930 (28/11)	Renfrewshire, Eastern	613	W.O. Brown	4,818	13.1
1931 (7/5)	Glasgow, St. Rollox	570	Miss E. Campbell	3,521	15.8
1931	Edinburgh, East	555	Rev. T.T. Alexander	2,872*	9.4
	Glasgow, St. Rollox	570	Miss E. Campbell	4,021	13.3
	Inverness	596	J.M. MacCormick	4,016	14.0
	Renfrewshire, Eastern	613	W.O. Brown	6,498	13.9
	Renfrewshire, Western	614	R.E. Muirhead	3,547*	11.0
1932 (17/3)	Dunbartonshire	591	R. Gray	5,178	13.4
1932 (28/6)	Montrose Burghs	577	D. Emslie	1,996*	11.7
1933 (2/2)	Fife, Eastern	592	E. Linklater	1,083*	3.6
1933 (2/11)	Kilmarnock	585	Sir A.M. MacEwen[1]	6,098	16.9
1935	Greenock	574	J.L. Kinloch	1,286*	3.3
	Kilmarnock	585	T.W. Campbell	2,346*	6.2
	Dunbartonshire	591	R. Gray	3,841*	7.8
	Inverness	596	J.M. MacCormick	4,273	16.1
	Western Isles	598	Sir A.M. MacEwen	3,704	28.1
	Renfrewshire, Eastern	613	W.O. Brown	6,593*	10.4
	Renfrewshire, Western	614	R.E. Muirhead	3,609*	11.3
	Combined Scottish Universities [3]	632	Prof. A.D. Gibb	3,865	14.2

Scottish National Party

1936 (31/1)	Combined Scottish Universities	632	Prof. A.D. Gibb	9,034	31.1
1936 (18/3)	Dunbartonshire	591	R. Gray	2,599*	6.2
1937 (10/6)	Glasgow, Hillhead	565	J.M. MacCormick	1,886*	9.0
1938 (25/2)	Combined Scottish Universities	632	Prof. A.D. Gibb	5,246	18.2
1940 (10/4)	Argyll	583	W. Power	7,308	37.2
1944 (17/2)	Kirkcaldy Burghs	575	D.C.C. Young	6,621	41.3
1945 (12/4)	Motherwell	603	†Dr. R.D. McIntyre	11,417	51.4
1945	Aberdeen, North	548	A.W. Walker	2,021*	5.3
	Dundee [2]	552	A. Donaldson	7,776*	4.6
	Edinburgh, East	555	F.C. Yeaman	2,149*	6.3
	Glasgow, Kelvingrove	566	C.M. Grieve	1,314*	4.9
	Kirkcaldy Burghs	575	D.C.C. Young	5,811	17.0
	Motherwell	603	Dr. R.D. McIntyre	8,022	26.7
	Perth	612	J.B. Brown	1,547*	4.3
	Renfrewshire, Western	614	R.B. Wilkie	1,955*	6.3
1946 (12/2)	Glasgow, Cathcart	561	Dr. W.O.G. Taylor	2,700*	10.4
1946 (5/12)	Kilmarnock	585	G. Dott	2,932*	7.8
1947 (27/11)	Edinburgh, East	555	Mrs. M. Dott	1,682*	5.0
1948 (7/10)	Stirling and Falkirk Burghs	579	R. Curran	2,831*	8.2
1950	Stirling and Falkirk Burghs	612	R. Curran	1,698*	3.7
	Motherwell	638	Dr. R.D. McIntyre	3,892*	9.3
	Perth and East Perthshire	646	D. Stewart	4,118*	9.3
1951	Western Isles	633	M.I. MacLean	820*	5.0
	Perth and East Perthshire	646	Dr. R.D. McIntyre	6,479	14.9
1952 (17/7)	Dundee, East	582	D. Stewart	2,931*	7.4
1955	Stirling and Falkirk Burghs	612	J. Halliday	2,885*	6.7
	Perth and East Perthshire	646	Dr. R.D. McIntyre	9,227	22.8
1959	Aberdeen North	579	W.A. Milne	2,964*	5.8
	Stirling and Falkirk Burghs	612	J. Halliday	2,983*	6.6
	Hamilton	636	D.R. Rollo	2,586*	6.2
	Kinross and West Perthshire	645	A. Donaldson	3,568	15.0
	Perth and East Perthshire	646	Dr. R.D. McIntyre	9,637	23.1
1961 (16/11)	Glasgow, Bridgeton	592	I.C.H. Macdonald	3,549	18.7
1962 (14/6)	West Lothian	653	W.C. Wolfe	9,750	23.3
1962 (22/11)	Glasgow, Woodside	608	A. Niven	2,562*	11.1
1963 (7/11)	Kinross and West Perthshire	645	A. Donaldson	1,801*	7.3
1963 (21/11)	Dundee, West	583	Dr. J.C. Lees	3,285*	7.4
1963 (12/12)	Dumfriesshire	626	J.H.D. Gair	4,001*	9.7
1964	Aberdeen, South	580	J.B. Reid	2,197*	4.4
	Glasgow, Springburn	606	A. McIntosh	2,366*	9.2

	Glasgow, Woodside	608	Dr. D.J.D. Stevenson	1,600*	5.4
	Kirkcaldy Burghs	610	Dr. J.C. Lees	4,423*	10.9
	Stirling and Falkirk Burghs	612	W.A. Milne	4,526*	10.0
	Aberdeenshire, East	613	B.M. Cockie	1,925*	6.3
	Dumfriesshire	626	J.H.D. Gair	5,726*	12.2
	Dunbartonshire, West	628	A. Gray	5,004*	12.0
	Fife, East	629	J. Braid	2,635*	6.8
	Rutherglen	640	R.N. Armstrong	1,648*	4.6
	Kinross and West Perthshire	645	A. Donaldson	3,522	14.1
	Perth and East Perthshire	646	Dr. R.D. McIntyre	7,186	17.4
	Roxburghshire, Selkirkshire and Peeblesshire	650	A.J.C. Kerr	1,093*	2.5
	Clackmannan and East Stirlingshire	651	C.D. Drysdale	5,106*	12.2
	West Lothian	653	W.C. Wolfe	15,087	30.4
1966	Dunfermline Burghs	584	J.A. Cook	5,304	15.0
	Edinburgh, South	590	H.M. Robertson	2,856*	7.3
	Glasgow, Craigton	596	G.A. Leslie	3,425*	9.4
	Glasgow, Maryhill	601	H. MacDonald	3,387*	11.5
	Glasgow, Shettleston	605	W. Lindsay	3,732*	12.1
	Glasgow, Springburn	606	W.J. Murton	2,222*	9.4
	Glasgow, Woodside	608	R.C. Fairlie	1,916*	7.2
	Kirkcaldy Burghs	610	Dr. J.C. Lees	5,223	13.4
	Stirling and Falkirk Burghs	612	W.A. Milne	6,322	14.4
	Aberdeenshire, East	613	B.M. Cockie	2,584*	8.9
	Dumfriesshire	626	J.H.D. Gair	5,727	12.6
	Dunbartonshire, East	627	W. Johnston	5,715*	9.0
	Dunbartonshire, West	628	R.O. Campbell	6,042	14.6
	Fife, East	629	J. Braid	5,394	14.4
	Fife, West	630	R.R. Patrick	6,046	14.1
	Lanark	637	H.C.D. Rankin	5,838*	10.1
	Rutherglen	640	A. Peacock	2,194*	6.4
	Midlothian	641	A.W.S. Rae	7,974	16.3
	Kinross and West Perthshire	645	A. Donaldson	4,884	20.5
	Perth and East Perthshire	646	M.B. Shaw	6,128	15.6
	Clackmannan and East Stirlingshire	651	C.D. Drysdale	8,225	20.1
	West Stirlingshire	652	Dr. R.D. McIntyre	9,381	26.0
	West Lothian	653	W.C. Wolfe	17,955	35.3
1967 (9/3)	Glasgow, Pollok	602	G.A. Leslie	10,884	28.2
1967 (2/11)	Hamilton	636	†Mrs. W.M. Ewing	18,397	46.0
1969 (30/10)	Glasgow, Gorbals	597	T. Brady	3,671	25.0
1970 (19/3)	South Ayrshire	622	S.H. Purdie	7,785	20.4

Scottish National Party

1970				
Aberdeen, North	579	J. McKenna	3,756*	8.4
Aberdeen, South	580	B.M. Cockie	2,777*	5.3
Coatbridge and Airdie	581	W. Brown	2,667*	6.0
Dundee, East	582	I. Macaulay	4,181*	8.9
Dundee, West	583	J.A. Shepherd	4,441*	8.7
Dunfermline Burghs	584	J.A. Cook	3,657*	9.7
Edinburgh, Central	585	Mrs. C.M. Moore	1,666*	8.0
Edinburgh, East	586	Mrs. H.B. Davidson	3,502*	8.2
Edinburgh, Leith	587	Miss M.G. Thomson	1,827*	7.0
Edinburgh, Pentlands	589	A.W.S. Rae	2,814*	5.9
Edinburgh, South	590	Dr. D.J.D. Stevenson	2,861*	6.9
Edinburgh, West	591	Miss M.M. Gibson	3,711*	6.8
Glasgow, Bridgeton	592	G. Wallace	1,550*	8.8
Glasgow, Central	595	A. McIntosh	1,688	14.0
Glasgow, Craigton	596	R.G. Edwards	2,946*	7.9
Glasgow, Gorbals	597	T. Brady	1,089*	7.4
Glasgow, Govan	598	J.M.T. Grieve	2,294*	10.3
Glasgow, Hillhead	599	Rev. G. Wotherspoon	1,957*	8.2
Glasgow, Maryhill	601	A.C.W. Aitken	3,273*	11.4
Glasgow, Pollok	602	G.A. Leslie	3,733*	8.9
Glasgow, Provan	603	W. McRae	4,181*	9.8
Glasgow, Scotstoun	604	A. Mitchell	4,313*	9.3
Glasgow, Shettleston	605	W. Lindsay	3,995	13.4
Glasgow, Springburn	606	W.J. Morton	3,323	14.3
Glasgow, Woodside	608	D.R. Rollo	1,912*	8.4
Kirkcaldy Burghs	610	Dr. J.C. Lees	4,863*	11.8
Paisley	611	Mrs. M. Macdonald	3,432*	7.3
Stirling and Falkirk Burghs	612	I.M. Murray	6,571	14.5
Aberdeenshire, East	613	A.R. Farquhar	9,377	29.8
Aberdeenshire, West	614	J.G. McKinlay	2,112*	5.3
North Angus and Mearns	615	J.A. McGugan	4,677	16.9
South Angus	616	Dr. C.G.M. Slesser	8,409	23.1
Argyll	617	I.S.M. MacCormick	9,039	29.9
Ayr	618	L. Anderson	2,186*	5.2
Bute and North Ayrshire	619	Mrs. M. Macrae	3,852*	11.0
Central Ayrshire	620	Rev. A. Macdonald	2,383*	5.1
Kilmarnock	621	A. MacInnes	2,836*	6.9
South Ayrshire	622	S.H. Purdie	3,103*	8.0
Banffshire	623	H. Watt	5,006	22.9
Berwickshire and East Lothian	624	Dr. D.R.F. Simpson	4,735*	10.2
Caithness and Sutherland	625	D.G. Barr	3,690	15.5

	Dumfriesshire	626	J.H.D. Gair	6,211	13.4
	Dunbartonshire, East	627	G.S. Murray	8,257*	11.3
	Dunbartonshire, West	628	R.O. Campbell	5,414*	12.0
	Fife, East	629	J. Braid	4,666*	11.8
	Fife, West	630	J. Halliday	5,386*	11.0
	Inverness	631	Miss A.C. Cameron	2,781*	7.1
	Ross and Cromarty	632	G. Nicholson	2,268*	11.7
	Western Isles	633	†D.J. Stewart	6,568	43.1
	Galloway	634	A. Donaldson	5,723	20.5
	Bothwell	635	T. McAlpine	6,157	12.7
	Hamilton	636	Mrs. W.M. Ewing	16,849	35.1
	Lanark	637	H.C.D. Rankin	7,859*	11.7
	Motherwell	638	Miss I. Lindsay	3,861*	9.9
	Lanarkshire, North	639	J.B. Hutchison	3,486*	8.2
	Midlothian	641	G. Park	9,047	15.6
	Moray and Nairnshire	643	T.A. Howe	7,885	27.8
	Kinross and West Perthshire	645	Mrs. E.Y. Whitley	4,670	18.6
	Perth and East Perthshire	646	D.C. Murray	7,112	17.0
	Renfrewshire, East	647	J.M. Buchanan	3,733*	6.7
	Renfrewshire, West	648	W.J.A. Macartney	4,195*	8.8
	Roxburghshire, Selkirkshire and Peeblesshire	650	H. Hastie	3,147*	6.8
	Clackmannan and East Stirlingshire	651	I.C.H. Macdonald	7,243	15.5
	West Stirlingshire	652	Dr. R.D. McIntyre	8,279	21.4
	West Lothian	653	W.C. Wolfe	15,620	28.2
1971 (16/9)	Stirling and Falkirk Burghs	612	Dr. R.D. McIntyre	13,048	34.6
1973 (1/3)	Dundee, East	582	R.G. Wilson	13,270	30.2
1973 (8/11)	Edinburgh, North	588	W.C. Wolfe	3,526	18.9
1973 (8/11)	Glasgow, Govan	598	†Mrs. M. Macdonald	6,360	41.9
1974 (F)	Aberdeen, North	553	J.A. McGugan	11,337	23.3
	Aberdeen, South	554	A. Stronach	7,599	13.7
	Coatbridge and Airdrie	555	D.R.M. Hill	7,961	17.3
	Dundee, East	556	†R.G. Wilson	20,066	39.5
	Dundee, West	557	J. Fairlie	12,959	25.1
	Edinburgh, Central	558	A.W.S. Rae	4,074	13.6
	Edinburgh, East	559	G.C. MacDougall	7,128	15.4
	Edinburgh, Leith	560	H. Miller	6,569	21.1
	Edinburgh, North	561	J. Lynch	4,550	12.7
	Edinburgh, Pentlands	562	T.T. Forrest	5,491*	12.4
	Edinburgh, South	563	R. Shirley	5,770	12.8
	Edinburgh, West	564	Mrs. C.M. Moore	4,241*	9.9

Scottish National Party

1974 (F) (cont.)					
Glasgow, Cathcart	565	A. Ewing	5,410	13.6
Glasgow, Central	566	S.M. Ewing	2,211	13.8
Glasgow, Craigton	567	R.G. Houston	6,303	17.9
Glasgow, Garscadden	568	M. MacRury	8,789	21.8
Glasgow, Govan	569	Mrs. M. Macdonald	9,783	40.9
Glasgow, Hillhead	570	K.S. Bovey	3,702*	11.3
Glasgow, Kelvingrove	571	C.M. MacKellar	5,666	19.2
Glasgow, Maryhill	572	A. McIntosh	8,920	24.9
Glasgow, Pollok	573	M.D'A. Conyers	6,584	14.4
Glasgow, Provan	574	R.G. Edwards	7,367	19.6
Glasgow, Queen's Park	575	D.G. MacKellar	4,394	15.6
Glasgow, Shettleston	576	W. Lindsay	5,834	22.0
Glasgow, Springburn	577	W.J. Morton	7,672	22.8
Greenock and Port Glasgow	578	J.K. Wright	4,881*	11.5
Motherwell and Wishaw	579	G. Nicholson	7,852	20.0
Paisley	580	D.R. Rollo	10,455	21.3
Stirling, Falkirk and Grangemouth	581	Dr. R.D. McIntyre	17,886	34.5
Aberdeenshire, East	582	†D. Henderson	18,333	50.8
Aberdeenshire, West	583	N. Suttar	6,827	15.4
North Angus and Mearns	584	H.C.D. Rankin	6,837	23.3
South Angus	585	Dr. C.G.M. Slesser	15,179	36.7
Argyll	586	†I.S.M. MacCormick	15,646	49.0
Ayr	587	C.D. Calman	4,706*	11.0
Bute and North Ayrshire	588	J.A. Murphy	6,104	16.3
Central Ayrshire	589	L. Anderson	7,255	15.1
Kilmarnock	590	A. MacInnes	7,644	15.3
South Ayrshire	591	R. Mullin	6,612	16.4
Banffshire	592	†H. Watt	11,037	46.1
Berwickshire and East Lothian	593	Dr. D.R.F. Simpson	6,956	14.2
Caithness and Sutherland	594	E.A.C. Sutherland	3,814	16.1
Dumfriesshire	595	L.A.B. Whitley	9,186	18.6
Dunbartonshire, Central	596	A.P. Welsh	5,906	14.5
Dunbartonshire, East	597	Mrs. M.A. Bain	11,635	22.3
Dunbartonshire, West	598	A. Murray	11,144	27.2
Fife, Central	599	D.V. Livingstone	10,324	22.5
Dunfermline	600	R.R. Patrick	8,695	17.8
Fife, East	601	J. Braid	8,593	19.5
Kirkcaldy	602	R.T. Knox	12,311	25.7
Inverness	603	R.M. Gibson	7,816	17.9
Ross and Cromarty	604	W. McRae	5,037	23.0

	Western Isles	605	†D.J. Stewart	10,079	67.1
	Galloway	606	G.H. Thompson	9,308	30.6
	Bothwell	607	G.A. Fisher	6,710	14.1
	East Kilbride	608	D.P. Macquarrie	13,819	25.9
	Hamilton	609	I.C.H. Macdonald	12,692	31.9
	Lanark	610	T. McAlpine	8,803	21.8
	Lanarkshire, North	611	Mrs. P. Watt	8,187	18.5
	Rutherglen	612	Mrs. L. Leslie	6,089	15.2
	Midlothian	613	J.G. McKinlay	19,450	27.0
	Moray and Nairnshire	614	†Mrs. W.M. Ewing	16,046	49.3
	Kinross and West Perthshire	616	D.C. Murray	6,274	23.1
	Perth and East Perthshire	617	G.D. Crawford	12,192	27.2
	Renfrewshire, East	618	Mrs. S.M. Watterson	5,268*	10.4
	Renfrewshire, West	619	C.D. Cameron	8,394	15.2
	Roxburghshire, Selkirkshire and Peeblesshire	620	Dr. D. Purves	3,953*	8.0
	Clackmannan and East Stirlingshire	621	†G.N. Reid	22,289	43.5
	West Stirlingshire	622	Mrs. J.T. Jones	12,886	29.7
	West Lothian	623	W.C. Wolfe	21,690	35.0
1974 (O)	Aberdeen, North	553	J.A. McGugan	13,509	29.7
	Aberdeen, South	554	A. Stronach	10,481	20.1
	Coatbridge and Airdrie	555	D.R.M. Hill	12,466	27.9
	Dundee, East	556	†R.G. Wilson	22,120	47.7
	Dundee, West	557	J. Fairlie	16,678	35.1
	Edinburgh, Central	558	A.W.S. Rae	6,866	24.8
	Edinburgh, East	559	G.C. MacDougall	11,213	25.6
	Edinburgh, Leith	560	R.J.D. Scott	7,688	26.1
	Edinburgh, North	561	J. Lynch	7,681	23.5
	Edinburgh, Pentlands	562	J.B. Hutchison	10,189	24.6
	Edinburgh, South	563	R. Shirley	9,034	21.7
	Edinburgh, West	564	Mrs. C.M. Moore	8,135	20.2
	Glasgow, Cathcart	565	A. Ewing	6,292	16.5
	Glasgow, Central	566	B. Nugent	2,790	19.2
	Glasgow, Craigton	567	R.G. Houston	8,171	24.3
	Glasgow, Garscadden	568	K.S. Bovey	12,100	31.2
	Glasgow, Govan	569	Mrs. M. Macdonald	9,440	41.0
	Glasgow, Hillhead	570	G.R. Borthwick	6,897	22.8
	Glasgow, Kelvingrove	571	C.D. Calman	6,274	23.2
	Glasgow, Maryhill	572	A. McIntosh	10,171	29.9
	Glasgow, Pollok	573	D.P. Macquarrie	10,441	24.3
	Glasgow, Provan	574	R.G. Edwards	10,628	30.2

Scottish National Party

1974 (O)	Glasgow, Queen's Park	575	D.G. MacKellar	5,660	21.8
(cont.)	Glasgow, Shettleston	576	R. Hamilton	7,042	28.5
	Glasgow, Springburn	577	W.J. Morton	9,049	28.3
	Greenock and Port Glasgow	578	J.K. Wright	9,324	21.1
	Motherwell and Wishaw	579	J. Mackay	12,357	31.9
	Paisley	580	D.R. Rollo	15,778	33.1
	Stirling, Falkirk and Grangemouth	581	Dr. R.D. McIntyre	20,324	39.8
	Aberdeenshire, East	582	†D. Henderson	16,304	48.5
	Aberdeenshire, West	583	N. Suttar	9,409	22.2
	North Angus and Mearns	584	I.M. Murray	9,284	34.2
	South Angus	585	†A.P. Welsh	17,073	43.8
	Argyll	586	†I.S.M. MacCormick	14,967	49.7
	Ayr	587	Miss E.A. Robinson	6,902	16.7
	Bute and North Ayrshire	588	J.A. Murphy	9,055	25.9
	Central Ayrshire	589	L. Anderson	11,533	24.5
	Kilmarnock	590	A. MacInnes	14,655	30.2
	South Ayrshire	591	R. Mullin	7,851	19.8
	Banffshire	592	†H. Watt	10,638	45.9
	Berwickshire and East Lothian	593	Dr. R.D. MacLeod	6,323	13.2
	Caithness and Sutherland	594	E.A.C. Sutherland	5,381	23.9
	Dumfriesshire	595	L.A.B. Whitley	12,542	26.4
	Dunbartonshire, Central	596	A.C.W. Aitken	11,452	29.1
	Dunbartonshire, East	597	†Mrs. M.A. Bain	15,551	31.2
	Dunbartonshire, West	598	A. Murray	13,697	33.7
	Fife, Central	599	D.V. Livingstone	14,414	33.4
	Dunfermline	600	Miss A.C. Cameron	13,179	28.6
	Fife, East	601	J. Braid	13,202	31.7
	Kirkcaldy	602	R.T. Knox	14,587	32.0
	Inverness	603	D.G. Barr	11,994	29.6
	Ross and Cromarty	604	W. McRae	7,291	35.7
	Western Isles	605	†D.J. Stewart	8,758	61.5
	Galloway	606	†G.H. Thompson	12,242	40.3
	Bothwell	607	J. McCool	11,138	24.5
	East Kilbride	608	G.S. Murray	19,106	36.7
	Hamilton	609	I.C.H. Macdonald	15,155	39.0
	Lanark	610	T. McAlpine	14,250	35.8
	Lanarkshire, North	611	Mrs. P. Watt	11,561	26.9
	Rutherglen	612	I.O. Bayne	9,732	25.3
	Midlothian	613	J.G. McKinlay	24,568	35.6
	Moray and Nairnshire	614	†Mrs. W.M. Ewing	12,667	41.2

Orkney and Shetland	615	H.N. Firth	3,025	17.2
Kinross and West Perthshire	616	D.P.B. Cameron	10,981	41.5
Perth and East Perthshire	617	†G.D. Crawford	17,337	40.8
Renfrewshire, East	618	I.S. Jenkins	11,137	23.2
Renfrewshire, West	619	C.D. Cameron	15,374	28.6
Roxburghshire, Selkirkshire and Peeblesshire	620	A. Edmonds	9,178	20.0
Clackmannan and East Stirlingshire	621	†G.N. Reid	25,998	50.7
West Stirlingshire	622	Mrs. J.T. Jones	16,331	38.2
West Lothian	623	W.C. Wolfe	24,997	40.9

[1] Also the candidate of the Scottish Party (q.v.)

SCOTTISH (PARLIAMENTARY) LABOUR PARTY

Formed at a conference held in Glasgow, August 1888. The word 'Parliamentary' was officially included in the name of the party but was not commonly used.
The party (of which Keir Hardie was secretary) held its final annual conference in December 1894 and shortly afterwards it merged into the Independent Labour Party.

Policy: Socialist.

Sources: Kellas, James G., *The Mid-Lanark By-Election (1888) and the Scottish Labour Party (1888–1894). Parliamentary Affairs,* Vol. XVIII (1964–65), pp. 318–329
Lowe, David, *Souvenirs of Scottish Labour.* 1919
Marwick, W.H., *A Short History of Labour in Scotland.* 1967
Pelling, Henry, *The Origins of the Labour Party 1880–1900.* 1965
*Labour Leader, February–August, 1889;
January 1893–September, 1922

Secessions: Dr. G.B. Clark (Caithness) who had been elected as a Liberal/Crofter; C.A.V. Conybeare (Camborne) and R.B. Cunninghame Graham (Lanarkshire, North-Western) who had been elected as Liberals advocating an advanced radical programme, all became associated with the party and held honorary offices. Graham contested the 1892 election as a party candidate but Clark and Conybeare were re-elected under Liberal auspicies and in January 1893 the SLP forced them to resign as vice-presidents by passing a resolution to debar members of other political parties holding office.

Elections:

1892	Dundee [2]	473	J. Macdonald	354	1.3
	Glasgow, Camlachie	482	R.B. Cunninghame Graham	906	11.9
	Glasgow, Tradeston	486	J.B. Burleigh	783	10.7
1894 (5/4)	Lanarkshire, Mid	521	R. Smillie	1,221	13.8

SCOTTISH PARTY

Formed in October 1932 by a group of moderate Scottish Nationalists opposed to certain policies of the National Party of Scotland. Agreement between the two parties was reached in March 1934 and they merged under the new title Scottish National Party, (q.v.).

Policy: Scottish nationalism.

Sources: Hanham, H.J., *Scottish Nationalism.* 1969
MacCormick, J.M., *The Flag in the Wind.* 1955.

Elections:

1933 (2/11)   Kilmarnock   585   Sir A.M. MacEwen[1]   6,098   16.9

[1] Also the candidate of the National Party of Scotland.

SCOTTISH PROHIBITION PARTY

Formed by Edwin Scrymgeour in Dundee, November 1901.
The party was disbanded in January 1935.

Policy: Prohibition of intoxicating drink.

Sources: *Scottish Prohibitionist*, 1906—23

Elections:

1908 (9/5)	Dundee	473	E. Scrymgeour	655	4.1
1910 (J)	Dundee [2]	473	E. Scrymgeour	1,512	4.8
1910 (D)	Dundee [2]	473	E. Scrymgeour	1,825	6.0
1917 (30/7)	Dundee	473	E. Scrymgeour	2,036	21.8
1918	Dundee [2]	552	E. Scrymgeour	10,423	15.1
1922	Dundee [2]	552	†E. Scrymgeour[1]	32,578	27.6
1923	Dundee [2]	552	†E. Scrymgeour	25,753	25.1
1924	Dundee [2]	552	†E. Scrymgeour	29,193	23.5
1929	Dundee [2]	552	†E. Scrymgeour	50,073	29.2
1931	Dundee [2]	552	E. Scrymgeour	32,229	18.3

[1] From this election onwards Scrymgeour (a former Labour Party member) received considerable support from the local Labour Party who only put forward one candidate for the two seats.

SCOTTISH SOCIALIST FEDERATION

Formed at a conference of Scottish socialist societies in Edinburgh, December 1888. The Federation merged into the Independent Labour Party when it was formed in 1893.

Policy: Socialism.

Sources: Kellas, James G., *The Mid-Lanark By-Election (1888) and the Scottish Labour Party (1888–1894). Parliamentary Affairs,* Vol. XVIII (1964–65), pp. 318–329
Lowe, David, *Souvenirs of Scottish Labour.* 1919

Elections:

| 1892 | Edinburgh, Central | 474 | J. Wilson[1] | 434 | 7.3 |

[1] Also candidate of the Scottish United Trades Councils Labour Party, (q.v.).

SCOTTISH UNITED TRADES COUNCILS LABOUR PARTY

Formed in March 1892 at a conference in Glasgow of delegates from trades councils and socialist organisations. The party was dissolved in March 1893 and branches were urged to join the newly formed Independent Labour Party.

Policy: Socialism.

Sources: Buckley, Kenneth D., *Trade Unionism in Aberdeen 1878 to 1900.* 1955
Marwick, W.H., *A Short History of Labour in Scotland.* 1967

Elections:

1892					
	Aberdeen, South	470	H.H. Champion	991	15.8
	Edinburgh, Central	474	J. Wilson[1]	434	7.3
	Glasgow, College	484	R. Brodie	225	2.1
	Stirlingshire	535	R.C. Robertson	663	6.3

[1] Also candidate of the Scottish Socialist Federation, (q.v.).

SOCIAL CREDIT PARTY OF GREAT BRITAIN

Formed by John G. Hargrave in the autumn of 1935, the party had its origins in an organisation founded by Hargrave in 1920 called Kibbo Kift which later became known as the Green Shirt Movement for Social Credit. The party was disbanded in 1950.

Policy: Social Credit.

Sources: *Front Line,* 1932–33

Elections:

1935	Leeds, South	155	W. Townend	3,642*	11.0
1950	Stoke Newington and Hackney North	40	J.G. Hargrave	551*	0.9

SOCIAL DEMOCRATIC FEDERATION

Formed, as the Democratic Federation, by H.M. Hyndman in June 1881. Re-named Social Democratic Federation, February 1884 and Social Democratic Party in July 1907. In September-October 1911 the Federation merged into a new party, the British Socialist Party (q.v.). In June 1916, pro-war members of the BSP, led by Hyndman, broke away to form the National Socialist Party (q.v.) which in August 1920 reverted back to the name Social Democratic Federation. The Federation was affiliated to the Labour Party from 1900—01 and from 1920 until it was dissolved in October 1939.

Policy: At first radical and then socialist from 1883.

Sources: Lee, H.W. & Archbold, E., *Social Democracy in Great Britain*. 1935
               Tsuzuki, C., *H.M. Hyndman and British Socialism*. 1961
               *Justice, 1884—1925
               *Social Democrat, 1925—39

Elections:

1885	Hampstead	20	J.E. Williams	27	0.6
	Lambeth, Kennington	28	J. Fielding	32	0.5
	Nottingham, West	154	J. Burns	598	5.4
1892	Bethnal Green, North-East	3	H.R. Taylor	106	2.0
	Salford, South	168	W.K. Hall	553	7.5
1895 (14/5)	Newington, Walworth	34	G. Lansbury	347	6.8
1895	Newington, Walworth	34	G. Lansbury	203	3.8
	Burnley	83	H.M. Hyndman	1,498	12.4
	Northampton [2]	150	F.G. Jones	1,216	6.7
	Salford, South	168	H.W. Hobart	813	10.8
1896 (22/2)	Southampton	178	C.A. Gibson	274	2.4
1898 (25/7)	Reading	163	H. Quelch	270	3.1
1900	Tower Hamlets, Bow and Bromley	49	G. Lansbury[1]	2,558	36.7
	West Ham, South	195	W.J. Thorne[1]	4,439	44.2
1902 (28/1)	Dewsbury	99	H. Quelch	1,597	13.6
1906	Bradford, East	76	E.R. Hartley	3,090	22.8
	Burnley	83	H.M. Hyndman	4,932	32.5
	Northampton [2]	150	J.E. Williams	2,544	11.7
	Northampton [2]	150	J. Gribble	2,366	10.9
	Southampton [2]	178	H. Quelch	2,146	8.0
	Camborne	225	J.J. Jones	109	1.5
	Accrington	296	D.D. Irving	4,852	38.3
	Aberdeen, North	469	T. Kennedy	1,935	25.1
1908 (24/4)	Manchester, North-West	143	D.D. Irving	276	2.6
1908 (1/8)	Shoreditch, Haggerston	43	H. Burrows	986	17.7

1908 (25/9)	Newcastle upon Tyne	149	E.R. Hartley	2,971	10.4
1910 (J)	Shoreditch, Haggerston	43	H. Burrows	701	11.1
	Bradford, East	76	E.R. Hartley	1,740	12.0
	Burnley	83	H.M. Hyndman	4,948	30.2
	Carlisle	88	A.C. Bannington	777	11.3
	Northampton [2]	150	J. Gribble	1,792	7.7
	Northampton [2]	150	H. Quelch	1,617	7.0
	Rochdale	164	D.D. Irving	1,755	12.6
	Sheffield, Brightside	173	C. Lapworth	510	4.7
	Aberdeen, North	469	T. Kennedy	1,344	16.9
1910 (D)	Burnley	83	H.M. Hyndman	3,810	23.8
	Rochdale	164	D.D. Irving	1,901	14.5

For election results between 1911 and 1916 see under
British Socialist Party. For elections between 1916 and
1920 see under National Socialist Party.

1921 (4/3)	Kirkcaldy Burghs	575	†T. Kennedy[1]	11,674	53.4
1922	Burnley	104	†D.D. Irving[1]	17,385	39.1
	Kirkcaldy Burghs	575	T. Kennedy[1]	12,089	48.6
1923	Islington, South	27	†W.S. Cluse[1]	7,764	37.0
	Islington, West	28	†F. Montague[1]	7,955	41.4
	Burnley	104	†D.D. Irving[1]	16,848	37.8
	Buckingham	279	E.J. Pay[1]	11,824	47.0
	Kirkcaldy Burghs	575	†T. Kennedy[1]	14,221	54.4
1924	Islington, South	27	†W.S. Cluse[1]	10,347	42.8
	Islington, West	28	†F. Montague[1]	10,174	45.3
	Buckingham	279	E.J. Pay[1]	8,939	30.6
	Kirkcaldy Burghs	575	†T. Kennedy[1]	14,038	52.7

After 1924 the Federation, probably through lack of
money, ceased to sponsor parliamentary candidates.
Cluse, Kennedy and Montague were all re-elected at the
General Election of 1929 but their candidatures were
sponsored by the local Labour Parties.

[1] Secured Labour Party endorsement

SOCIALIST LABOUR PARTY

Formed in 1903 after a split in the Social Democratic Federation (q.v.) when part of its Scottish membership broke away and formed a new party based on the American Socialist Labour Party. In April 1920 some members and branches (subsequently expelled for their action) formed a Unity Committee with other socialist organisations and merged into the Communist Party (q.v.). The party was still active in Scotland until the early 1950's but it is likely that it has now been dissolved.

Policy: Socialism.

Sources: Beer, Max, *A History of British Socialism. Volume 2.* 1953
             Cole, G.D.H., *British Working Class Politics 1832–1914.* 1941
             Cole, G.D.H., *A History of the Labour Party from 1914.* 1948
             Kendall, Walter, *The Revolutionary Movement in Britain 1900–21.* 1969
             The Socialist, 1902–24 and 1939–50

Elections:

1918	Halifax	132	A. McManus	4,036	15.4
	Manchester, Gorton	180	J.T. Murphy	1,300*	6.7
	Ince	381	W. Paul	2,231	13.0

SOCIALIST PARTY OF GREAT BRITAIN

Formed in London in June 1904 after a split in the Social Democratic Federation (q.v.).
Like the Socialist Labour Party (q.v.) it was modelled on the lines of the American
Socialist Labour Party.

Policy: Socialism.

Sources: Beer, Max, *A History of British Socialism. Volume 2.* 1953
                Cole, G.D.H., *British Working Class Politics 1832–1914.* 1941
                Cole, G.D.H., *A History of the Labour Party from 1914.* 1948
                Kendall, Walter, *The Revolutionary Movement in Britain 1900–21.* 1969
                Socialist Standard, 1904–

Elections:

1945	Paddington, North	37	C. Groves	472*	1.7
1946 (20/11)	Paddington, North	37	C. Groves	286*	1.2
1950	Paddington, North	32	G. McClatchie	192*	0.5
	East Ham, South	131	H. Young	256*	0.7
1953 (3/12)	Paddington, North	32	W.E. Waters	242*	0.9
1959	Bethnal Green	5	J.L. Read	899*	2.4
1962 (22/11)	Glasgow, Woodside	608	R. Vallar	83*	0.4
1964	Bromley	102	E.S. Grant	234*	0.6
	Glasgow, Woodside	608	R. Vallar	88*	0.3
1966	Hampstead	19	H.G. Baldwin	211*	0.4
	Glasgow, Woodside	608	R. Vallar	122*	0.5
1970	Wandsworth, Clapham	42	F.W. Simkins	220*	0.7
	Hornsey	158	E.S. Grant	156*	0.4
1974 (O)	Camden, Hampstead	17	R.O. Critchfield	118*	0.3

UNITED DEMOCRATIC PARTY

Formed during the early summer of 1974. The party was formed by a number of candidates who had contested the February 1974 General Election as Independents or Independent Conservatives. The leader of the party is James E. Tippett, an insurance and finance broker from Bridgwater, Somerset.

Policy: Right-wing Conservatism.

Sources: None traced.

Elections:

1974 (O)	Hillingdon, Ruislip-				
	Northwood	51	Mrs. W. Hobday	458*	1.1
	Bath	100	J.V. Kemp	150*	0.3
	Cambridge	139	C.J. Curry	885*	1.7
	Stroud	372	J.S. Churchill	241*	0.4
	Petersfield	378	P.H.H. Bishop	117*	0.2
	Norfolk, South	430	C.C. Fairhead	317*	0.5
	Bridgwater	453	S.R. Harrad	288*	0.5
	Somerset, North	454	J.F. Poling	387*	0.5
	Taunton	455	L.D. Bradford	283*	0.6
	Wells	456	Miss P. Howard	778*	1.4
	Weston-super-Mare	457	E.P. Iszatt	296*	0.5
	Yeovil	458	J.E. Tippett	332*	0.6
	Chippenham	489	E.J. Johns	278*	0.5

UNITED EMPIRE PARTY

Formed by Lord Beaverbrook in February 1930. The following month as the result of assurances given by the Prime Minister, Stanley Baldwin, Beaverbrook decided to disband the party and return subscriptions. However, Viscount Rothermere (who had supported Beaverbrook in the formation of the party) decided, against Beaverbrook's wishes, to keep the party in existence and broaden the scope of its policy. At the General Election of 1931 the party pledged itself to support National Government candidates and it appears to have been disbanded shortly after the election.

Policy: (Beaverbrook)   Empire free-trade.

               (Rothermere)   Imposition of high import duties on all manufactured goods; adequate subsidies for farmers; ruthless economy in public expenditure; no more surrenders in India; no diplomatic relations with Moscow.

Sources: *Daily Express, 1930—31*

            Daily Mail, 1930—31

Elections:

1930 (2/9)	Bromley	103	V.C. Redwood	9,483	24.1
1930 (30/10)	Paddington, South	38	Mrs. A.N. Stewart-Richardson[1]	494*	1.7
1931 (19/2)	Islington, East	25	A.C. Critchley[2]	8,314	27.2

[1] Candidate of the local branch but the party's headquarters refused to support her and gave their help to a candidate sponsored by the Empire Free Trade Crusade.

[2] Also candidate of the Empire Free Trade Crusade.

VECTIS NATIONALIST PARTY

Formed in Ryde, Isle of Wight, November 1969. The word 'Vectis' is the old Roman name for the Isle of Wight.

Policy: Independence for the Isle of Wight with status similar to the Isle of Man.

Sources: *Isle of Wight County Press,* 1969—

Elections:

| 1970 | Isle of Wight | 404 | R.W.J. Cawdell | 1,607* | 2.8 |

WOMEN'S PARTY

Formed, as the Women's Social and Political Union, by Mrs. Emmeline Pankhurst in Manchester, October 1903. Re-named Women's Party, November 1917. The party was disbanded early in 1919.

Policy: At first the party advocated militant action to secure the extension of the franchise to women. During the General Election of 1918 the party broadly supported the policy of Lloyd George and the Coalition Government.

Sources: Mitchell, David, *Women on the Warpath.* 1966
      Suffragette, 1912—15
      Britannia, 1915—18

Elections:

| 1918 | Smethwick | 230 | Miss C. Pankhurst | 8,614 | 47.8 |

WORKERS' PARTY OF SCOTLAND

Formed in Edinburgh in the early autumn of 1966 by a number of former members of the Communist Party of Great Britain.

Policy: Communism (Marxist—Leninist); the creation of a Socialist Republic of Scotland.

Sources: *Scottish Vanguard*, 1966—

Elections:

1969 (30/10)	Glasgow, Gorbals	597	M. Lygate	72*	0.5

WORKERS REVOLUTIONARY PARTY

Formed, as the Socialist Labour League, May 1959. Name changed to Workers Revolutionary Party (the British Section of the International Committee of the Fourth International), November 1973.

Policy: Communism (Trotskyist).

Sources: *Workers Press,* 1969—

Elections:

1974 (F)	Lambeth, Central	62	S.G. Smart	337*	1.1
	Newham, North-East	71	Miss V. Redgrave	760*	1.7
	Birmingham, Stechford	114	R.P. Bull	280*	0.6
	Liverpool, Toxteth	202	W. Hunter	263*	0.9
	Pontefract and Castleford	238	B. Lavery	991*	2.2
	Swindon	277	Mrs. K.M. Blakeney	240*	0.5
	Wallsend	289	D. Temple	1,108*	1.6
	Merthyr Tydfil	522	R.J. Battersby	160*	0.5
	Dunbartonshire, Central	596	S.J. Hammond	52*	0.1
1974 (O)	Hackney, North and Stoke Newington	37	M.A. Van der Poorten	159*	0.6
	Hillingdon, Hayes and Harlington	50	R.P. Bull	198*	0.5
	Lambeth, Central	62	S.G. Smart	233*	0.9
	Newham, North-East	71	Miss V. Redgrave	572*	1.5
	Coventry, North-East	146	A.A. Wilkins	352*	0.8
	Liverpool, Toxteth	202	J.S. Dillon	365*	1.4
	Pontefract and Castleford	238	T. Parsons	457*	1.1
	Swindon	277	Mrs. K.M. Blakeney	206*	0.4
	Wallsend	289	K. Flynn	435*	0.7
	Aberavon	538	A.J. Bevan	427*	0.9

Appendix 1

STATISTICAL SUMMARY

In calculating the average and the % vote per opposed candidate, votes cast in two-member constituencies have been counted as half votes.

By-election years are prefixed by an asterisk.

Page references are given within square brackets opposite the party name.

Election	Candidates (MPs)	Total Votes	Forfeited Deposits	Average Vote	Average % Vote
ACTION PARTY					**[1]**
1959	1	2,821	1	2,821	8.1
*1959–1964	2	1,762	2	881	3.5
1966	4	4,075	4	1,019	3.7
*1970–1974(F)	1	873	1	873	2.5
AGRICULTURAL PARTY					**[2]**
*1931–1935	1	4,404	0	4,404	14.6
ALL PARTY ALLIANCE					**[3]**
*1966–1970	4	8,572	3	2,143	6.1
ANTI-PARTITION OF IRELAND LEAGUE OF GREAT BRITAIN					**[4]**
1950	4	5,084	4	1,271	3.0
1951	1	1,340	1	1,340	2.7
ANTI-WASTE LEAGUE					**[5]**
*1918–1922	4 (2)	33,123	0	8,281	49.2
BRITISH EMPIRE PARTY					**[6]**
1951	1	1,643	1	1,643	3.4

Election	Candidates (MPs)	Total Votes	Forfeited Deposits	Average Vote	Average % Vote
BRITISH MOVEMENT					[7]
*1966–1970	1	282	1	282	3.0
1970	1	704	1	704	2.5
1974(F)	1	711	1	711	1.5
BRITISH NATIONAL PARTY					[8]
1964	1	3,410	1	3,410	9.1
1966	3	5,182	3	1,727	5.3
BRITISH PEOPLE'S PARTY					[9]
*1935–1945	1	576	1	576	2.6
*1945–1950	1	239	1	239	1.3
BRITISH SOCIALIST PARTY					[10–11]
*1910(D)–1918	3	4,536	–	1,512	11.1
1918	16	71,762	2	4,485	21.1
BRITISH UNION OF FASCISTS AND NATIONAL SOCIALISTS					[12]
*1935–1945	3	1,291	3	430	1.7
CAMPAIGN FOR SOCIAL DEMOCRACY					[13]
1974(F)	5 (1)	17,426	4	3,485	8.3
1974(O)	1	13,714	0	13,714	34.6
COMMON WEALTH					[14–15]
*1935–1945	12 (3)	98,089	0	8,174	36.6
1945	23 (1)	110,634	16	4,810	12.6
COMMONWEALTH LAND PARTY					[16]
1931	2	1,347	2	674	1.9

Election	Candidates (MPs)	Total Votes	Forfeited Deposits	Average Vote	Average % Vote
COMMUNIST PARTY OF ENGLAND (MARXIST–LENINIST)					[17]
*1970–1974(F)	2	237	2	119	0.7
1974(F)	6	1,419	6	237	0.6
1974(O)	8	1,320	8	165	0.4
COMMUNIST PARTY OF GREAT BRITAIN					[18–31]
*1918–1922	1	2,592	1	2,592	10.3
1922	5 (1)	33,637	1	6,137	27.4
1923	4	39,448	0	8,565	30.0
1924	8 (1)	55,346	1	6,397	25.2
*1924–1929	1	2,618	0	2,618	12.9
1929	25	50,634	21	1,902	5.4
*1929–1931	7	12,529	6	1,790	7.3
1931	26	74,824	21	2,680	8.1
*1931–1935	6	22,259	5	3,710	11.0
1935	2 (1)	27,117	0	13,559	37.8
*1935–1945	4	6,853	3	1,713	7.7
1945	21 (2)	102,780	12	4,664	14.6
*1945–1950	3	6,734	2	2,245	7.8
1950	100	91,765	97	9,177	2.0
*1950–1951	1	729	1	729	2.3
1951	10	21,640	10	2,164	4.7
*1951–1955	1	1,457	1	1,457	4.3
1955	17	33,144	15	1,950	4.9
*1955–1959	1	972	1	972	2.5
1959	18	30,896	17	1,716	4.3
*1959–1964	6	5,799	6	967	2.8
1964	36	46,442	36	1,290	3.5
1966	57	62,092	57	1,089	3.0
*1966–1970	6	4,802	6	800	2.9
1970	58	37,970	58	655	1.8
*1970–1974(F)	1	1,519	1	1,519	4.7
1974(F)	44	32,743	43	744	1.8
1974(O)	29	17,426	29	601	1.6
CO-OPERATIVE PARTY					[32]
*1910(D)–1918	1	2,832	–	2,832	24.9
1918	10 (1)	57,785	0	5,779	28.6

Election	Candidates (MPs)	Total Votes	Forfeited Deposits	Average Vote	Average % Vote
DEMOCRATIC PARTY [1]					[33]
1945	5	1,809	5	362	1.3
DEMOCRATIC PARTY [2]					[34]
*1966–1970	2	2,924	2	1,462	4.0
1970	5	15,292	4	3,058	5.6
EMPIRE FREE TRADE CRUSADE					[35]
*1929–1931	2 (1)	19,523	0	9,762	32.3
FELLOWSHIP PARTY					[36]
1959	1	1,189	1	1,189	2.6
1964	1	1,112	1	1,112	2.5
1966	1	906	1	906	2.1
*1966–1970	1	34	1	34	0.4
*1970–1974(F)	1	792	1	792	3.6
HIGHLAND LAND LEAGUE					[37]
1918	4	8,710	1	2,178	19.2
INDEPENDENT DEMOCRATIC ALLIANCE					[38]
1974(F)	6	1,976	6	329	0.7
INDEPENDENT LABOUR PARTY					[39–42]
*1892–1895	3	8,679	–	2,893	18.2
1895	28	44,325	–	1,230	11.5
*1895–1900	4	7,523	–	1,881	22.1
*1910(D)–1918	2	3,438	–	1,719	21.4
*1929–1931	1	12,293	0	12,293	33.3
1931	19 (3)	260,344	1	12,594	34.5
*1931–1935	4	16,966	2	4,242	13.1
1935	17 (4)	139,577	8	8,012	24.1
*1935–1945	11	55,453	1	5,041	25.3
1945	5 (3)	46,769	1	9,354	35.2

Election	Candidates (MPs)	Total Votes	Forfeited Deposits	Average Vote	Average % Vote
Independent Labour Party (Cont.)					
*1945–1950	4 (1)	8,367	3	2,092	10.7
1950	4	4,112	4	1,028	2.7
*1950–1951	2	1,366	2	683	2.0
1951	3	4,057	3	1,352	3.6
1955	2	3,334	2	1,667	5.0
*1955–1959	3	1,621	3	540	2.6
1959	2	923	2	462	1.8
*1959–1964	1	586	1	586	3.1
1966	1	441	1	441	0.9
1970	1	847	1	847	1.7

INDEPENDENT NUCLEAR DISARMAMENT ELECTION COMMITTEE [43]

1964	2	1,534	2	767	1.6

INDEPENDENT PARLIAMENTARY GROUP [44]

*1918–1922	7 (5)	70,351	3	9,258	40.6

INTERNATIONAL MARXIST GROUP [45]

1974(F)	3	716	3	239	0.5

IRISH CIVIL RIGHTS ASSOCIATION [46]

1974(O)	7	2,381	7	340	1.0

IRISH NATIONALIST MOVEMENT [47]

1885	2 (1)	3,489	–	1,745	38.7
1886	1 (1)	2,911	–	2,911	67.0
1892	1 (1)	2,537	–	2,537	65.3
1895	1 (1)	2,089	–	2,089	59.0
1900	1 (1)	2,044	–	2,044	57.9
1906	1 (1)	2,808	–	2,808	71.5
1910(J)	1 (1)	2,943	–	2,943	79.1
1910(D)	1 (1)	2,458	–	2,458	78.1

E

Appendix 1

Election	Candidates (MPs)	Total Votes	Forfeited Deposits	Average Vote	Average % Vote
Irish Nationalist Movement (Cont.)					
1918	2 (1)[1]	8,225	0	8,225	44.4
1922	2 (1)[1]	12,614	0	12,614	44.6
1923	2 (1)[1]	10,322	0	10,322	49.5
1924	1 (1)[1]	—	—	—	—
1929	1 (1)[1]	—	—	—	—
LABOUR INDEPENDENT GROUP					[48]
1950	5	26,014	2	5,203	14.0
LEAGUE OF EMPIRE LOYALISTS					[49]
*1955–1959	1	1,487	1	1,487	4.0
1964	3	1,046	3	349	0.9
LIVERPOOL PROTESTANT PARTY					[50]
1931	1	7,834	0	7,834	24.7
1935	1	6,677	0	6,677	24.5
1945	1	2,601	0	2,601	13.2
MEBYON KERNOW					[51]
1970	1	960	1	960	2.0
1974(F)	1	850	1	850	1.5
1974(O)	1	384	1	384	0.7
MUDIAD GWERINIAETHOL CYMRU					[52]
(Welsh Republican Movement)					
1950	1	613	1	613	1.3
NATIONAL DEMOCRATIC AND LABOUR PARTY					[53–54]
1918	27 (10)	193,065	6	7,151	34.4
*1918–1922	2	12,667	0	6,334	32.8

[1] Unopposed

Election	Candidates (MPs)	Total Votes	Forfeited Deposits	Average Vote	Average % Vote
NATIONAL DEMOCRATIC PARTY					**[55]**
1964	1	349	1	349	0.6
1966	1	769	1	769	1.3
1970	4	9,581	3	2,396	7.9
*1970–1974(F)	1	3,090	1	3,090	7.6
1974(F)	1	1,161	1	1,161	1.6
NATIONAL FARMERS' UNION OF ENGLAND AND WALES					**[56]**
*1910(D)–1918	1	1,784	–	1,784	35.4
1918	6	23,124	3	3,854	23.3
1922	3	16,267	0	5,422	25.2
NATIONAL FEDERATION OF DISCHARGED AND DEMOBILIZED SAILORS AND SOLDIERS					**[57–58]**
*1910(D)–1918	1	794	–	794	26.3
1918	5	12,329	3	2,466	15.4
NATIONAL FELLOWSHIP					**[59]**
*1959–1964	1	4,834	0	4,834	19.0
NATIONAL FRONT					**[60–64]**
*1966–1970	1	1,400	1	1,400	5.6
1970	10	11,449	10	1,145	3.6
*1970–1974(F)	5	10,695	4	2,139	6.8
1974(F)	54	76,865	54	1,423	3.1
*1974(F)–					
1974(O)	1	1,713	1	1,713	11.5
1974(O)	90	113,843	90	1,265	3.1
NATIONAL INDEPENDENCE PARTY					**[65]**
*1970–1974(F)	2	1,211	2	606	1.7
1974(F)	1	1,373	1	1,373	4.4

Election	Candidates (MPs)	Total Votes	Forfeited Deposits	Average Vote	Average % Vote
NATIONAL LABOUR PARTY					[66]
1959	1	1,685	1	1,685	4.1
NATIONAL PARTY [1]					[67–68]
*1910(D)–1918	1	513	–	513	10.8
1918	26 (2)	94,389	11	3,630	20.6
*1918–1922	2	3,767	2	1,884	7.5
NATIONAL PARTY [2]					[69]
*1966–1970	1	517	1	517	1.2
NATIONAL PROHIBITION PARTY					[70]
*1922–1923	1	130	1	130	0.9
NATIONAL SOCIALIST PARTY					[71]
1918	4 (2)	26,230	1	6,558	28.3
NATIONAL UNION OF SMALL SHOPKEEPERS					[72]
*1955–1959	1	348	1	348	1.0
*1959–1964	1	886	1	886	2.7
*1966–1970	1	1,053	1	1,053	2.4
NEW CONSERVATIVE PARTY					[73]
*1959–1964	4	3,127	4	782	2.3
NEW PARTY					[74–75]
*1929–1931	1	4,472	0	4,472	16.0
1931	24	36,377	22	1,516	4.1
PATRIOTIC PARTY					[76]
1964	2	1,108	2	554	1.5
1966	1	126	1	126	0.4

Election	Candidates (MPs)	Total Votes	Forfeited Deposits	Average Vote	Average % Vote
PEOPLE					[77]
1974(F)	6	4,576	6	763	1.7
1974(O)	5	1,996	5	399	0.9
PEOPLE'S LEAGUE FOR THE DEFENCE OF FREEDOM					[78]
*1955–1959	1	2,730	1	2,730	12.2
PLAID CYMRU					[79–84]
1929	1	609	1	609	1.6
1931	2	2,050	1	1,025	16.1
1935	1	2,534	1	2,534	6.9
*1935–1945	3	14,464	0	4,821	21.2
1945	7	16,017	6	2,288	9.1
*1945–1950	2	12,775	0	6,388	24.7
1950	7	17,580	6	1,044	6.8
1951	4	10,920	4	2,730	6.1
*1951–1955	2	10,243	1	5,122	13.7
1955	11	45,119	7	4,102	11.3
*1955–1959	3	10,646	3	3,549	8.4
1959	20	77,571	14	3,879	10.3
*1959–1964	3	5,305	3	1,768	6.1
1964	23	69,507	21	3,022	8.4
*1964–1966	1	1,551	1	1,551	6.7
1966	20	61,071	18	3,054	8.7
*1966–1970	3 (1)	40,520	0	13,507	39.8
1970	36	175,016	25	4,862	12.4
*1970–1974(F)	1	11,852	0	11,852	37.0
1974(F)	36 (2)	171,374	26	4,760	11.7
1974(O)	36 (3)	166,321	26	4,620	11.6
RADICAL ALLIANCE					[85]
*1964–1966	1	253	1	253	0.5
1966	1	163	1	163	0.5
REVOLUTIONARY COMMUNIST PARTY					[86]
*1935–1945	1	1,781	1	1,781	4.6

Election	Candidates (MPs)	Total Votes	Forfeited Deposits	Average Vote	Average % Vote
SCOTTISH LABOUR PARTY					[87]
1900	1	3,107	—	3,107	41.7
*1900–1906	2	6,884	—	3,442	24.8
1906	5	14,877	—	2,975	22.9
*1906–1910(J)	2	5,951	—	2,976	27.2
SCOTTISH LAND RESTORATION LEAGUE					[88]
1885	5	2,359	—	472	5.9
SCOTTISH NATIONAL PARTY					[89–97]
*1924–1929	1	842	1	842	4.5
1929	2	3,313	2	1,657	5.2
*1929–1931	3	10,866	1	3,622	13.0
1931	5	20,954	2	4,191	12.3
*1931–1935	4	14,355	2	3,589	11.4
1935	8	29,517	5	3,690	12.2
*1935–1945	7 (1)	44,111	2	6,302	27.8
1945	8	30,595	6	3,338	9.1
*1945–1950	4	10,145	4	2,536	7.9
1950	3	9,708	3	3,236	7.4
1951	2	7,299	1	3,650	10.0
*1951–1955	1	2,931	1	2,931	7.4
1955	2	12,112	1	6,056	14.8
1959	5	21,738	3	4,348	11.3
*1959–1964	6	24,948	4	4,158	12.9
1964	15	64,044	12	4,270	10.6
1966	23	128,474	10	5,586	14.1
*1966–1970	4 (1)	40,737	0	10,184	29.9
1970	65 (1)	306,802	43	4,720	12.8
*1970–1974(F)	4 (1)	36,204	0	9,051	31.4
1974(F)	70 (7)	633,180	7	9,045	22.7
1974(O)	71 (11)	839,617	0	11,826	30.6
SCOTTISH (PARLIAMENTARY) LABOUR PARTY					[98]
1892	3	2,043	—	681	8.0
*1892–1895	1	1,221	—	1,221	13.8

Election	Candidates (MPs)	Total Votes	Forfeited Deposits	Average Vote	Average % Vote
SCOTTISH PARTY					[99]
*1931–1935	1	6,098	0	6,098	16.9
SCOTTISH PROHIBITION PARTY					[100]
*1906–1910(J)	1	655	–	655	4.1
1910(J)	1	1,512	–	˙756	2.4
1910(D)	1	1,825	–	913	3.0
*1910(D)–1918	1	2,036	–	2,036	21.8
1918	1	10,423	0	5,212	7.6
1922	1 (1)	32,578	0	16,289	13.8
1923	1 (1)	25,753	0	12,877	12.6
1924	1 (1)	29,193	0	14,597	11.8
1929	1 (1)	50,073	0	25,037	14.6
1931	1	32,229	0	16,115	9.2
SCOTTISH SOCIALIST FEDERATION					[101]
1892	1	434	–	434	7.3
SCOTTISH UNITED TRADES COUNCILS LABOUR PARTY					[102]
1892	4	2,313	–	578	7.9
SOCIAL CREDIT PARTY OF GREAT BRITAIN					[103]
1935	1	3,642	1	3,642	11.0
1950	1	551	1	551	0.9
SOCIAL DEMOCRATIC FEDERATION					[104–105]
1885	3	657	–	219	2.2
1892	2	659	–	330	4.8
*1892–1895	1	347	–	347	6.8
1895	4	3,730	–	781	8.4
*1895–1900	2	544	–	272	2.8
1900	2	6,997	–	3,499	40.5
*1900–1906	1	1,597	–	1,597	13.6
1906	8	21,974	–	2,306	16.9
*1906–1910(J)	3	4,233	–	1,411	10.2

Election	Candidates (MPs)	Total Votes	Forfeited Deposits	Average Vote	Average % Vote
Social Democratic Federation (Cont.)					
1910(J)	9	15,184	—	1,498	11.8
1910(D)	2	5,711	—	2,856	19.2
*1918–1922	1 (1)	11,674	0	11,674	53.4
1922	2 (1)	29,474	0	14,737	43.9
1923	5 (4)	58,612	0	11,722	43.5
1924	4 (3)	43,498	0	10,875	42.9

SOCIALIST LABOUR PARTY   [106]

1918	3	7,567	1	2,522	11.7

SOCIALIST PARTY OF GREAT BRITAIN   [107]

1945	1	472	1	472	1.7
*1945–1950	1	286	1	286	1.2
1950	2	448	2	224	0.6
*1951–1955	1	242	1	242	0.9
1959	1	899	1	899	2.4
*1959–1964	1	83	1	83	0.4
1964	2	322	2	161	0.5
1966	2	333	2	167	0.5
1970	2	376	2	188	0.6
1974(O)	1	118	1	118	0.3

UNITED DEMOCRATIC PARTY   [108]

1974(O)	13	4,810	13	370	0.7

UNITED EMPIRE PARTY   [109]

*1929–1931	3	18,291	1	6,097	17.7

VECTIS NATIONALIST PARTY   [110]

1970	1	1,607	1	1,607	2.8

WOMEN'S PARTY   [111]

1918	1	8,614	0	8,614	47.8

Election	Candidates (MPs)	Total Votes	Forfeited Deposits	Average Vote	Average % Vote
WORKERS' PARTY OF SCOTLAND					[112]
*1966–1970	1	72	1	72	0.5
WORKERS REVOLUTIONARY PARTY					[113]
1974(F)	9	4,191	9	466	1.0
1974(O)	10	3,404	10	340	0.9

Appendix 2

CAMPAIGN FOR A MORE PROSPEROUS BRITAIN

At the General Election of October 1974, Tom Keen a property developer from Oldham launched a campaign to oust the Labour Government. Keen and three of his associates contested a total of twenty-five constituencies not seeking votes for themselves but urging electors to vote anything but Labour or Communist.

1974 (O)					
	Redbridge, Ilford South	75	T.L. Keen	169*	0.4
	Wandsworth, Battersea South	90	T.L. Keen	170*	0.6
	Wandsworth, Putney	91	T.L. Keen	125*	0.3
	Aldridge-Brownhills	94	T.L. Keen	210*	0.4
	Birmingham, Handsworth	107	T.L. Keen	105*	0.3
	Birmingham, Perry Barr	110	T.L. Keen	86*	0.2
	Birmingham, Yardley	115	T.L. Keen	111*	0.2
	Bolton, East	121	H. Smith	149*	0.3
	Bradford, West	128	H. Smith	339*	0.8
	Coventry, South-West	149	T.L. Keen	144*	0.3
	Derby, North	152	H. Smith	242*	0.4
	Huddersfield, West	179	H. Smith	136*	0.3
	Keighley	183	C.W. Deakin	179*	0.4
	Manchester, Moss Side	212	H. Smith	96*	0.3
	Middleton and Prestwich	216	H. Smith	234*	0.4
	Portsmouth, North	240	T.L. Keen	527*	1.0
	Preston, North	242	H. Smith	138*	0.3
	Preston, South	243	H. Smith	87*	0.2
	Walsall, South	291	T.L. Keen	150*	0.4
	York	304	H. Smith	304*	0.5
	Gravesend	398	T.L. Keen	239*	0.4
	Chorley	403	H. Smith	185*	0.3
	Loughborough	419	H. Smith	125*	0.2
	Sowerby	516	H. Smith	157*	0.4
	Glasgow, Govan	569	T. Clyde	27*	0.1

Candidates:	25
Total votes:	4,434
Forfeited deposits:	25
Average vote:	177
Average % vote:	0.4

Appendix 3

SERVICEMEN CANDIDATES

At five by-elections between November 1961 and June 1962, a total of nine 'Independent Servicemen' candidates were nominated but in most cases took no active part in the election campaigns. By becoming parliamentary candidates they obtained their release from H.M. Forces for the cost of a forfeited deposit. As a result of these candidatures new regulations were introduced which prevented Servicemen from automatically obtaining their discharge.

1961 (22/11)	Dorset, South	360	P.O. Burn	181*	0.4
			M. Fudge	82*	0.2
			J.C. O'Connor	45*	0.1
1961 (22/11)	Norfolk, Central	447	J. Andrews	79*	0.2
1961 (22/11)	Northamptonshire, South	455	P.B. Buchan	332*	0.9
1961 (22/11)	Wiltshire, Chippenham	514	K. Jerrome	260*	0.7
			J.P. Naylor	237*	0.6
			M.J.A. Smith	88*	0.2
1962 (6/6)	Middlesbrough, West	210	M. Thompson	117*	0.3

Candidates:	9
Total votes:	1,421
Forfeited deposits:	9
Average vote:	158
Average % vote:	0.4

INDEX TO PARTIES AND ORGANISATIONS

Main entries are indicated by the use of bold type. References to footnotes are denoted by 'n' placed after the page number.

INDEX TO NAMES

References to footnotes are denoted by 'n' placed after the page number.